THE FAILURE OF BRITISH FASCISM

The Failure of British Fascism

The Far Right and the Fight for Political Recognition

Edited by

Mike Cronin
History Research Fellow
Sheffield Hallam University

First published in Great Britain 1996 by
MACMILLAN PRESS LTD
Houndmills, Basingstoke, Hampshire RG21 6XS
and London
Companies and representatives
throughout the world

A catalogue record for this book is available
from the British Library.

ISBN 0-333-64674-6

 First published in the United States of America 1996 by
ST. MARTIN'S PRESS, INC.,
Scholarly and Reference Division,
175 Fifth Avenue,
New York, N.Y. 10010

ISBN 0-312-15963-3

Library of Congress Cataloging-in-Publication Data
The failure of British fascism : the far right and the fight for
political recognition / edited by Mike Cronin.
p. cm.
Includes bibliographical references (p.   ) and index.
ISBN 0-312-15963-3 (cloth)
1. Fascism—Great Britain—History—20th century. 2. Great
Britain—politics and government—20th century. 3. British Union of
Fascists—History. 4. Left and right (Political science)
I. Cronin, Mike.
DA578.F28   1996
320.5'33'0941—dc20   95-52407
                                                                CIP

Selection, editorial matter and Chapter 1© Mike Cronin 1996
Chapters 2-10 © Macmillan Press Ltd 1996

All rights reserved. No reproduction, copy or transmission of
this publication may be made without written permission.

No paragraph of this publication may be reproduced, copied or
transmitted save with written permission or in accordance with
the provisions of the Copyright, Designs and Patents Act 1988,
or under the terms of any licence permitting limited copying
issued by the Copyright Licensing Agency, 90 Tottenham Court
Road, London W1P 9HE.

Any person who does any unauthorised act in relation to this
publication may be liable to criminal prosecution and civil
claims for damages.

10 9 8 7 6 5 4 3 2 1
05 04 03 02 01 00 99 98 97 96

Printed and bound in Great Britain by
Antony Rowe Ltd, Chippenham, Wiltshire

Contents

List of Contributors		vii
Preface		ix
1	Introduction: 'Tomorrow We Live' – The Failure of British Fascism? *Mike Cronin*	1
2	The Extreme Right in the 1920s: Fascism in a Cold Climate, or 'Conservatism with Knobs on'? *David Baker*	12
3	State Management of the British Union of Fascists in the 1930s *Richard Thurlow*	29
4	Oswald Mosley and the Union Movement: Success or Failure? *Anne Poole*	53
5	The Conservative Party, the British Extreme Right and the Problem of Political Space, 1967–83 *Martin Durham*	81
6	The Esoteric Ideology of the National Front in the 1980s *Roger Eatwell*	99
7	Contemporary Fascism in the Local Arena: The British National Party and 'Rights for Whites' *Nigel Copsey*	118
8	British Fascism: The Ugly Duckling *Roger Griffin*	141

| 9 | British Fascism Revisited: A Failure of Imagination?
Kenneth Lunn | 166 |

Index 181

List of Contributors

David Baker is a Senior Lecturer in Politics at Nottingham Trent University. He is also Co-Director of the 'Members of Parliament Project' with Professor Andrew Gamble and Dr Steve Ludlam of Sheffield University. He has published widely in the fields of fascism and conservatism in Britain. Amongst other research projects, he is currently working on a book on the life and ideas of A.K. Chesterton, and an edited volume on Britain and the politics of the European Union.

Nigel Copsey is Lecturer in European Studies (Politics) at University College Stockton-on-Tees, a college of the University of Teesside. He has recently completed his doctoral thesis on the extreme right in contemporary France and Britain.

Mike Cronin is History Research Fellow at Sheffield Hallam University. He has published widely on the subject of the extreme right Blueshirt movement in Ireland. At present he is working on a history of Ireland for Macmillan, and a general history of sport and nationalism in Ireland.

Martin Durham is Senior Lecturer in Politics at the University of Wolverhampton. He has published extensively on the politics of the right in Britain and the USA and is currently working on a book on women and fascism.

Roger Eatwell is Senior Lecturer in Politics at the University of Bath. Recent publications include: *Fascism – A History* (1995, editor with A.W. Wright), *Contemporary Political Ideologies* (1993), and numerous articles and chapters on aspects of fascism and neo-fascism. He is currently completing a book on European political culture.

Roger Griffin is Principal Lecturer in History at Oxford Brookes University and has written and lectured widely on historical and contemporary aspects of ultra-nationalism, especially fascism. His publications include *The Nature of Fascism* (1991; 1993), *Fascism* (1995), as well as contributions to *Contemporary Political*

Ideologies (eds R. Eatwell and A. Wright, 1993), *Fascism and Theatre: Comparative Studies on the Aesthetics and Politics of Performance in Inter-war Europe* (ed. G. Berhaus, 1995) and *Fascism outside Europe* (ed. S.U. Larsen, forthcoming).

Kenneth Lunn lectures in the Social and Cultural History Department at the University of Portsmouth. He has published widely on the subject of British fascism and minorities in Britain.

Anne Poole teaches Politics at Kingston University and is presently working on a detailed study of the post-1945 thought of Oswald Mosley.

Richard Thurlow is a lecturer in the Department of History at the University of Sheffield. He is the author of *Fascism in Britain: A History, 1918–85* (1987) and *The Secret State: British Internal Security in the Twentieth Century* (1994).

Preface

The chapters included in this book emerged from a conference, *The Failure of British Fascism*, staged at Sheffield Hallam University in May 1994. The impetus for organizing a conference on such a topic came from the success and later failure of Derek Beackon's stand as a British National Party candidate in the Millwall ward of Tower Hamlets Council. The elections in Millwall had been accompanied by huge media interest in the rise of a fascist party. Within public circles there was a demand to understand how such a candidate could achieve a popular mandate in the British electoral system, and concerns were expressed that such a victory could be the precursor to a rise of the Far Right as has happened in other parts of Europe.

This book charts the troubled history of fascism and the Far Right in Britain, and explain its constant ebb and flow between some level of success and its more normal condition of failure. Every major movement from the 1920s through to the British National Party in the 1990s is assessed, and conclusions drawn, not only on the fascist movements themselves, but on the inherent strengths and weaknesses of the British political system which prevents fascism from breaking through. Without some understanding of this unique ideological phenomenon from the past how can we hope to understand its current and future developments? Despite a general consensus in the public mind that fascism was a pre-1945 experience, fascist and far right ideas, thinkers, activists and movements continue to exist and influence the political landscape in Britain.

This book was a joint effort and thus I would like to thank the contributors for their prompt delivery of their chapters, all done with good humour despite the constant pressure which was put upon them to produce quickly. The excellent work of John Hope and Christopher Husbands, who spoke at the original conference yet were unable to contribute to the book, should not go unnoticed. In Sheffield the help and encouragement of all my colleagues and administrative staff was of vital importance, particularly that of Mick Worboys who allowed the necessary time and funding to organize the conference and produce the book, and Dave Mayall who gave excellent and much needed advice throughout. Roger Griffin at Oxford Brookes University must take the blame for bringing me into the fascinating world of fascist studies. Gráinne Twomey at Macmillan deserves special thanks for seeing the potential of this book, and for answering all the ridiculous questions which an editor poses throughout the production of a final text. At home, my wife Jayne Harris lived with the failure of British fascism for far too long, but always provided unrelenting encouragement. All these people remain without fault, and any errors which remain in the book are my sole responsibility.

Mike Cronin
Sheffield, May 1995

1 Introduction: 'Tomorrow We Live' – The Failure of British Fascism?
Mike Cronin

In 1938 Sir Oswald Mosley, leader of Britain's most famous fascist grouping, the British Union of Fascists (BUF), wrote a short book, *Tomorrow We Live*. He concluded:

> In divine purpose the spirit of man rises above and beyond the welter of chaos and materialism to the conquest of a civilisation that shall be the sum and the glory of the travail of the ages. In that high fate tomorrow we live.
> (Mosley, 1938, p. 72)

Mosley's apocalyptic view of Britain at the end of the 1930s was a Dantesque vision of a society, corrupted by a multitude of forces, standing on the brink of a terrible war. This, Mosley believed, would produce a cleansing political reawakening for the martial spirit of the nation. For Mosley in the pre-war period, and for British fascism throughout the century, the synthesis of corrupting influences which have been consistently predicted by the fascists, thereby bringing about a mass support base and propelling fascism to power, have simply not emerged. It appears that the glorious fascistized tomorrow which Mosley dreamt of, and which would give British fascism life, has not materialized. Fascism in Britain has failed to take political power, tomorrow has never come, and the ideology waits dormant, like Frankenstein's monster, without the life force which Mosley envisaged.

The claim that British fascism has failed is, however, a naively simple statement, which denies the potential threat that fascism could pose in the future. Political events in the period 1993-5 demonstrate well the dichotomy which exists when fascism is perceived to threaten British society. On the one hand fascism, despite its historic tradition of failure in this country, could, as in other nations, break through. On the other, no matter what form fascism may take, the strength of the British system will preclude any breakthrough. The victory of the British National Party (BNP) in a Millwall Council election in 1993 was accompanied by a high level of press excitement and a feeling that Britain was about to see the beginning of a resurgence of fascism in line with events in Italy, France and the former Soviet bloc. The panic passed when the BNP failed to hold the seat in May 1994. The ensuing period saw the media and anti-fascist groups switch their attention from the party itself to the actual issue of fascist and racist violence, as personified by the Combat 18 group. In March 1995 a *World In Action* programme (27 March 1995) highlighted the activities of Combat 18. This in turn led to a Parliamentary question from Greville Janner. He asked whether there were the 'resources and the determination to deal with these awful people', and was requesting that action be taken against Combat 18. Janner drew comparisons between the activities of that group and the atrocities committed by the Nazis during the Second World War. Janner personified the view that fascism was a constant threat. In his mind, and maybe for many others, Combat 18 and fascism were indivisible, the threat of a breakthrough was still real, and the historical British *laissez-faire* attitude towards such a domestic threat was not adequate considering the gravity of the situation. In response, John Major condemned Combat 18 as a 'repellent organisation' (Hansard, 30/3/95, p. 1182), but placed faith in the argument that British society could always deal with any threat posed by fascism. Major believed that the Criminal Justice Act and the police would be able to contain any threat which was posed by Combat 18 and its followers. In short, Major was essentially stressing an attitude towards British fascism which has prevailed throughout the century – that although fascism was a menace to British society, the threat which it posed could always be managed by the institutions of the state. Failure for British fascism, according to this standpoint, is not only a historical, but a terminal condition.

The chapters in this book offer a highly relevant national study of the experience of the different fascist groupings throughout the century. To view British fascism in terms of failure is not a new idea (Stevenson, 1990; Eatwell, 1992). What is important about this book is a new approach that allows for an evaluation of all the different fascist movements in Britain up to the present day. The agenda of the book utilizes the combined knowledge of the different contributors who are all building not only on an expertise of specific movements but also on a wider and multidisciplinary knowledge of fascism in terms of empirical, definitional and comparative study. The book aims to unravel the reasons behind fascism's failure (and its limited successes), while evaluating the impact of many wider issues which have affected both the development of British fascism and its legacy in British society.

Despite its failure to mount a successful and sustained challenge at the electoral level, fascism has been a constant force in Britain throughout the twentieth century. The major movements were the British Fascists of the 1920s, the BUF during the 1930s, Mosley's Union Movement of the 1950s, the National Front (NF) which spanned the 1960s and 1970s, and most recently the BNP. These are the movements which receive the bulk of attention in this book as they were the most visible and most supported organizations. There were, however, many other movements which have existed such as the British People's Party (1939–45), the Greater Britain Movement (1964–7), the Imperial Fascist League (1928–40), the League of Empire Loyalists (1948–67), the National Socialist Movement (1962–8) and the British Movement (1968–83). The existence of such a wide range of movements demonstrates that fascism in Britain, despite the popular imagery which equates fascism with Nazism and the Holocaust (and therefore dismisses it as an electable ideology), has always had its organizers and followers and to some is very much alive. These activists have never relented in their goals of popularizing their agenda and bringing their message into the political arena.

There are questions which need to be addressed if the experience of British fascism is to be understood. Although failure is an idea that has been widely used before, we need to question what is actually meant by this, for how are we to understand fascism's failure in Britain if it is multifaceted? Do the reasons for failure lie with the fascist ideology itself or do they lie within the complex structure of the British sociopolitical system?

Three key elements dominate the book: the nature of British political society, an understanding of fascism and notions of failure. The boundaries of these, plus the conundrums and difficulties which are inevitably present within such, are more specifically defined in the contributors' work.

THE NATURE OF BRITISH POLITICAL SOCIETY

There has been a tendency in the popular mind to believe that the experience of the Second World War taught society a valuable lesson which would never allow fascism to reassert itself. However, it is not an ideology which is locked in a time capsule belonging to the inter-war years, but moreover something which has attempted to reinvent and repackage itself on many occasions and in numerous guises. In recent years we have witnessed the sceptre of resurgent fascism across the globe, on occasions operating within the parliamentary system as with Le Pen's Front National, and yet on others operating outside the system (often accompanied by virulent racism and the threat of violence) as with the Afrikaner Weerstandsbeweging (AWB) in South Africa. In Britain the attitude towards fascism, or rather the threat of it, has been in the main low key. This of course raises questions which are concerned with the very nature of the British political psyche.

In countries other than Britain during the twentieth century there have been certain common experiences which are seen as precursors to the rise of fascism (e.g. Mosse, 1979; Robinson, 1989). Such experiences are commonly viewed as some form of emergency, crisis or breakdown which befell the liberal system of democracy. These have an impact to a greater or lesser degree on class relationships, the economy, national boundaries or national identity, which in turn bring about a new or revitalized form of revolutionary politics in the fascist form. These elements are seen to have been present and predominant in inter-war Italy, Germany, Spain and Portugal, thereby leading to fascist regimes. The impact in countries such as Romania, Belgium and France was less acute, but still led to the presence of high profile and well supported fascist movements.

The fascist movements in Britain have never formed a regime, and cannot be compared to the success achieved by the high profile movements such as the Iron Guard in Romania, the Rexists in Belgium or the Parti Populaire Français in France. Nor did British fascism have the chance to achieve the back-door route to power, that of collaboration, which was so common to other fledgling fascist movements across Europe during the Second World War. However, the fascist movements in Britain have achieved varying levels of support and success. The fact that there have been crises or some sense of threat to British society in the twentieth century is undeniable. Britain has not always been the gloriously cosy and tranquil nation envisaged by J.B. Priestley in his *English Journey* (Priestley, 1933). For all the contributors in the book there is some feeling of crisis or threat to society which impacted on the fascist movement under consideration. In the 1920s the threat was international communism and the Jewish conspiracy. The BUF was fired by the effects of the world-wide depression on Britain. The Union Movement attempted to capitalize on a nation struggling to come to terms with post-war reconstruction and the future of Britain within Europe. The NF throughout the 1960s, 1970s and 1980s attempted to feed off popular concerns over immigration, economic uncertainties and the changing world order. Most recently the BNP has attempted to gain political capital from the race issue and the chaos of the post-Thatcherite legacy. British fascism has not therefore suffered from a lack of society's ills on which it could build, though paradoxically it has failed to make enough political capital from these ills to propel itself into a position of dominance and ascendancy. The nature of Britain's political society has always counteracted against any breakthrough by British fascism. Why is this? Generally, there has been a feeling that, among other factors, the strength of the British parliamentary system, the nature of the electoral system, the existence of a predominantly 'right' wing Conservative Party and the rejection of alien political ideologies by British society would counter fascism's revolutionary thrust. Society has always managed to keep the fascist threat in check. The specifics of these factors which operated against and controlled fascism can be seen in the different chapters. David Baker, Anne Poole and Martin Durham clearly illustrate why fascism suffered from a lack of political space and why they could not vanquish those traditions of the political system which have traditionally operated against them. Richard Thurlow demonstrates how fascism was tightly controlled by the state thereby preventing any real level of success. Finally, Roger Eatwell shows that the esoteric ideas of the NF during the 1980s are not compatible with the British tradition of rejecting alien political cultures. Britain, it seems, provides an example of special national circumstances and traditions which operate against fascism's search for a popular support base and political success.

AN UNDERSTANDING OF FASCISM

To judge whether or not fascism as an ideology, irrespective of other forces, is tendentially bound to failure is a highly taxing dilemma. Fascism is a complex and problematic philosophy to characterize. Through the decades there have been countless definitional works attempting to explain the main tenets of fascism (e.g. De Felice and Ledeen, 1976; Griffin, 1991; Mosse, 1979; Payne, 1980), as well as the numerous attempts to understand the development of fascism in the different nations of Europe and the wider world (e.g. for German inter-war fascism see Heiden and Farquharson, 1983; for Italian inter-war fascism see Gentile, 1975, and Zunino, 1985; and for post-war European fascism see Cheles, Ferguson and Vaughan, 1991). The tendency of fascism to defy a consensus definition creates problems for a collection such as this. Many writers would question, as Roger Griffin does in Chapter 9, whether the British experience of fascism can indeed sit within any of the previous definitonal understandings of fascism gained from wider comparative studies. The book then requires some sense of commonality, i.e. what we label as fascist. Compromise is met by highlighting some universal elements of the movements discussed in each chapter.

(a) The movements under consideration have either applied the term fascist to themselves or have openly embraced the ideologies of previous fascist movements or regimes from around the world.

(b) Despite the constant use of the electoral platform by the different fascist groups, they have repeatedly (and openly) remained suspicious of the democratic system, and thus are characteristically anti-liberal and anti-democratic.

(c) The dominant themes which recur in the ideological and political campaigns of the different groups constantly stress

Introduction

common issues such as race, nationalism, anti-liberalism, the use of violence and an appeal to youth, among many other issues, which have traditionally been seen as central to the definition of fascism since the works of the 1960s (e.g. Rogger and Weber, 1965; Weber, 1965; and Woolf, 1966).

(d) Although lacking the classic charismatic figurehead to inspire the leader cult so prevalent in many other varieties of fascism, and having been quite rightly dismissed as sawdust Caesars and tinpot Führers (Thurlow, 1987, p. 301), the men at the forefront of British fascism are vitally important in our use of the term. Considering the number of different movements in existence throughout the twentieth century, the leadership of British fascism has revolved around five key interconnected figures: Arnold Leese, A.K. Chesterton, Oswald Mosley, Colin Jordan and John Tyndall. Despite the populist window dressing used by them in an attempt to achieve popularity, all the leaders have constantly sought inspiration from fascism, and embraced its ideals.

It is important to state here that there has been a common usage of the term fascist with respect to all the movements under discussion by various academics (e.g. Lunn and Thurlow, 1980; Rees, 1979; Thurlow, 1987), we are therefore building on a tradition of general consensus. With this agreed, albeit generalized, definition we can move forward to concentrate on the specifics of this phenomenon, on how it has been seen, if at all, to fail.

NOTIONS OF FAILURE

The notion of failure is constantly referred to throughout the book, and despite being the *raison d'être* behind the various considerations of the different fascist groupings, it is a term which has many different, although equally valid, applications. With regard to fascist political groupings the measurement of failure has been used in three main ways throughout the text. First, at the power level we discuss fascism's failure to gain control of the institutions of the state. It is in this context that British fascism has resolutely failed. Second, regarding electoral and popular politics we question whether fascism has failed to gain any notable support. Here, while some groupings such as the Imperial Fascist League in the 1920s, the Union Movement in the 1950s and the British Movement in the 1970s failed to gain any sizeable electoral or popular support, others such as the BUF, the NF in the 1970s and the BNP in the 1990s did not. Indeed they have met with some considerable, if short-lived, success, gaining large numbers of followers and polling well in certain electoral districts. This type of success is discussed by Martin Durham in Chapter 5 with reference to the NF, and Nigel Copsey in Chapter 8 in terms of the BNP's recent performance. Third, in terms of influence we ask if fascism has failed to influence politics and society by acting as a catalyst for a wider debate of those issues which the fascists perceive to be important (e.g. immigration, race, the unreconstructed economy and morality). In this context British fascism has met with significant success because many of the causes which it has addressed have entered the political mindset with a vengeance. Mosley's ideas were applauded by Lord Rothermere and certain senior political figures. The NF saw many of their ideas echoed by those in the Monday Club. There were also accusations that the Liberal Democrats used ideas, such as opposing new housing for the Asian population, which had been espoused by the BNP in their campaigning in the Tower Hamlets local government elections of 1993. The success of fascists in influencing the mainstream political consciousness is a central theme in the chapters of Richard Thurlow, Martin Durham and Nigel Copsey. They all demonstrate clearly that the ideas and policies put forward by fascist groups can win a hearing in the political mainstream, and therefore come to influence and even direct (as with the Monday Club) 'respectable' political thinking.

The most important rationale behind this book is that fascism, despite its record of comparative failure, has been ever present in twentieth century Britain, and continues to exist. Fascism did not die in 1945. As Seton-Watson noted:

> The complexity of the legacy of fascism remains. Hitler and Mussolini were destroyed, and the Age of Fascism belongs to the past, but the world is full of their heirs.
> (Seton-Watson, 1979)

The contributors to this book have dealt with one of the thorniest philosophies of twentieth-century political history, and attempted to explain how it has operated and been received in Britain. There are obviously internal contradictions and disagreements within such an edited book, but this speaks volumes about the nature of the subject under consideration. What is at issue here is not just the fascist movements which have existed in Britain, but also the very nature of political failure and the traditions of British political society itself. Confusing the overall picture and negating any agreed conclusion as to the failure of British fascism are the changing identities and tactics of the fascists themselves. There is not one lineal trait which links the British Fascists of the 1920s with the BNP of the 1990s. The picture is confused by ideological changes, transformations in society, altering perceptions of fascism and the threat it poses, and the differing political strategies adopted by the movements in question. Sir Oswald Mosley and John Tyndall are separated by half a century, the images which their movements provoke are very different (Mosley's Blackshirts as opposed to Tyndall's skinheads), and the former was openly fascist, while the latter has largely hidden his fascist thinking behind electoral politics. Yet Tyndall, with different tactics, awaits with Mosley the glorified tomorrow which was outlined at the beginning. In 1988 Tyndall wrote *The Eleventh Hour: A Call for British Rebirth*:

> Our creed is one of heroism, and the coming epoch calls for the return of the heroic virtues. Not for us the cosy tranquillity of the political soft option; for us only the long march through the cold night – which must precede the glorious dawn ... Today, from out of the chaos and the ruins wrought by the old politics, new men are rising. These men of the new age are now working night and day across the land to forge the sinews of the movement to which their lives and mine are dedicated. Above them as they work are the spirits of legions of mighty ancestors whose bones lie at the bottom of the oceans and beneath the soil of five continents where the men and women of our blood have borne the British flag and stamped the mark of British genius. Today we feel the voices of these past generations calling down to us in sacred union, urging us to be worthy of their example and their sacrifice. To them we owe it to fight on, and to dare all, so that a great land and a great race may live again in splendour.
>
> (Tyndall, 1988)

Roger Griffin's poignant conclusion to his chapter turns around the question of failure and asks what conditions would allow fascism to succeed in Britain. This is a vitally important change to the original dilemma as it places the emphasis on British society rather than on fascism itself. Fascism has been an ever present force in British society since the end of the First World War. It has problematized the race and immigration issue, it has consistently used violence and has thus brought about a climate of fear in certain localized areas, and has at times shifted the centre of political debate to the right. Despite this, the conditions of the wider society have always prevented fascism from taking electoral power. While not attempting to deny that fascism has an effect on society, it has undoubtedly failed to gain a high and sustained level of electoral success. The credit for this lies with the nature and operation of British political society when fascism is perceived to threaten it. Fascism continues to exist in Britain in both its electoral form and its radical violent form. Fascism may have a history of failure in Britain, but a historical precedent does not govern the future.

REFERENCES

Cheles, L., Ferguson, R. and Vaughan, M., *Neo-Fascism in Europe* (London, 1991).
De Felice, R. and Ledeen, M., *Fascism: An Informal Introduction to its Theory and Practice* (New Brunswick, 1976).
Eatwell, R., 'Why has the extreme right failed in Britain?' in Hainsworth, P. (ed.), *The Extreme Right in Europe and the USA* (London, 1992).
Gentile, E., *Le origini dell'ideologia fascista* (Bari, 1975).
Griffin, R., *The Nature of Fascism* (London, 1991).
Heiden, J. and Farquharson, J., *Explaining Hitler's Germany* (London, 1983).
Lunn, K. and Thurlow, R., *British Fascism. Essays on the Radical Right in Inter-War Britain* (London, 1980).
Mosley, O., *Tomorrow We Live* (London, 1938).
Mosse, G.L., *International Fascism. New Thoughts and Approaches* (London, 1979).
Payne, S.G., *Fascism: Comparison and Definition* (Wisconsin, 1980).
Priestley, J.B., *English Journey* (London, 1933).
Rees, P., *Fascism in Britain. An Annotated Bibliography* (New Jersey, 1979).
Robinson, R.A.H., *Fascism in Europe, 1919–1945* (London, 1989).

Rogger, H. and Weber, E. (eds), *The European Right: A Historical Profile* (Berkeley, 1966).
Seton-Watson, H., 'The age of fascism and its legacy', in Mosse, G.L. (ed.), *International Fascism. New Thoughts and Approaches* (London, 1979).
Stevenson, J., 'Conservatism and the failure of fascism in interwar Britain', in Blinkhorn, M. (ed.), *Fascists and Conservatives. The Radical Right and the Establishment in Twentieth-Century Europe* (London, 1990).
Thurlow, R., *Fascism in Britain. A History, 1918–1985* (Oxford, 1987).
Tyndall, J., 'The Eleventh Hour: A Call for British Rebirth', excerpt taken from Griffin, R. (ed.), *Fascism* (Oxford, 1995).
Weber, E., *Varieties of Fascism* (New York, 1965).
Woolf, S.J. (ed.), *European Fascism* (London, 1968).
Zunino, P.G., *L'ideologia del fascismo* (Bologna, 1985).

2 The Extreme Right in the 1920s: Fascism in a Cold Climate, or 'Conservatism with Knobs on'?
David Baker

> No one wastes time in explaining why such quixotic and eccentric movements as the British Fascisti in the 1920s and the Imperial Fascist League in the 1930s, were minute elements on the political fringe.
> (Thurlow, 1989, p. 68)

In the light of the above entirely accurate sentiments, it might appear that in tackling the reasons behind the 'failure' of British fascism in the 1920s the present writer may be engaged in a supererogatory, or at least largely thankless, task. The manifest failure of the British fascists is well known. Mosley himself talked of throwing money down the 'political drain of British fascism' (Thurlow, 1989, p. 76). There is also a danger of 'yet further duplication of an already well told story' (Lunn, 1989, p. 140). But the time is ripe to bring together the latest thinking on this subject and, besides, as Michael Biddiss has pointed out:

> The history of ideas tolerates no general law suggesting that either influence or conscious sophistication stands directly proportionate to worth . . . prevalent error may be not infrequently more accurately representative of the spirit of an age than ultimately more profitable ideas . . .
> (Biddiss, 1977, p. 20)

The 1920s proved a propitious time for fascist and other 'radical right' movements in Europe. Between 1900 and 1918 many countries experienced considerable domestic social and political upheaval, offering the necessary political space for fascism[1] to take root. Destabilizing forces, such as the advent of mass politics, and pressure for further reform from democratizing forces, including considerable trade union and socialist agitation, were played out after 1917 against the background of the collapse of the Tsarist regime in the Russian Revolution. The aftermath of the First World War further destabilized the situation, causing challenges to established European elites (mainly aristocratic and conservative), often on a scale not witnessed since the French Revolution.

In countries like Italy and Germany, where loyalty to the liberal system among the ruling elites was highly conditional, some conservative elites sought uneasy alliances with these new and more extreme movements against their common enemies on the left. In the process new and increasingly influential movements of the right emerged combining populist parliamentary and extra-parliamentary activities. Prior to 1918 these forces were still contained by the existing elites, and lacking features such as a commitment to a 'corporate state', or a leader cult, they remained essentially pre-fascistic.

However, in the wake of the 1917 Bolshevik Revolution and a disastrous European war, with its aftermath of humiliating defeat for some nations, coupled with economic devastation and mass migration, more orthodox forms of conservatism were either destabilized or badly discredited and 'fascism' was able to emerge in its own right. In Italy, apart from the normal post-war dislocations and uncertainties, the sudden advent of virtually universal male suffrage and proportional representation propelled its ill-prepared Catholic and conservative ruling elites into the mass political arena. The result was political stagnation and an alliance of fundamentalist Catholic reaction with the new movements of populist authoritarianism to give rise to Mussolini's 'Fascist' regime. Consequently, the emergence of generic fascism throughout Europe was, as Martin Blinkhorn has suggested:

> Nourished by the new climate of crisis and the new climate of ideas ... groups, movements, and parties, operating on the margins of the established right proliferated during the 1920s and into the 1930s ... shriller in their nationalism, more plebeian in composition, less respectful of tradition and of established hierarchies, more violent in their behaviour,

and prepared to employ pseudo-leftist rhetoric... there was, in other words, a definite difference between these 'fascist' movements and their 'conservative' forerunners.

(Blinkhorn, 1990, pp. 5–6)

Yet, while mainland Europe in the 1920s was a hotbed of competing movements, parties and regimes of the authoritarian and illiberal right, Britain produced the 'damp squibs' of the fascist firmament, consisting of a small number of almost totally uninfluential movements, parties and propaganda vehicles. Indeed, there is some reasonable doubt amongst scholars that there were any 'true' fascist movements or parties operating in Britain before the 1930s. Robert Benewick set the trend when he insisted that 'there was little Fascist content' in the doctrine of the British Fascists before 1932 (Benewick, 1971, pp. 28–9; Griffiths, 1983, pp. 85–96).

Scholarly explanations for this failure of the early fascist movement in Britain have burgeoned in recent years, in the wake of earlier detailed research on the failure of the most successful fascist party, the British Union of Fascists (BUF) founded in 1932 by Sir Oswald Mosley. A wide diversity of explanatory factors has emerged from this historiography, giving rise, if not to agreement, to a broad consensus as to the causes of this failure. But before reviewing these factors, we must turn our attention to who the early British fascists were. Like its continental counterparts British fascism had deep roots in earlier movements of the 'radical right', particularly after 1880. Some of the most influential antecedents were particularly active in the Edwardian and early First World War period (Thurlow, 1987, pp. 14–15).

THE PRE-WAR 'RADICAL RIGHT' IN BRITAIN

Mainland Europe's social structure was especially favourable to populist appeals to authoritarianism; here a widespread revolt of the right was often spearheaded and orchestrated by powerful reactionary agrarian elites and supported by *petit bourgeois* and peasant strata who felt threatened by the process of modernization (Thurlow, 1987, pp. 2–3). However, in Britain both the peasant strata and the agrarian anti-modernizers were largely missing from the equation. Thus, Geoffrey Searle defines the 'radical right' in Edwardian Britain as a loose coalition of largely middle- and upper-class super-patriots, provoked into action by fears of imperial decline, constitutional imbalance (centred on the agitation over the Parliament Act of 1911) and increasing working-class unrest, particularly in the 1909–14 period. Such disaffected conservatives favoured extreme Ulster Unionism, tariff reform and compulsory military service. In the wake of the Marconi scandal of 1911 they also attacked 'aliens', intellectuals, Jews and orthodox political parties. Parliamentary democracy was also held under suspicion for being too weak to grapple with pressing national problems. Consequently, as Paul Kennedy says of the 'Diehard' faction of the radical right:

> They were in certain respects, forward looking, dissatisfied with negative Conservatism and optimistic about forging a link with the 'common man' . . . as well as an overlap with more orthodox Conservatism and in certain areas (interventionism by the state, dislike of *laissez faire* economics), with creeds of the Left. The Edwardian Right was, therefore, 'an extraordinary, and quite illogical amalgam of modernising and anti-modernising attitudes'.
> (Kennedy, 1981, p. 10; see also Dangerfield, 1970, pp. 50–1)

Of all the forces behind the British 'radical right', the 'Diehards' were arguably the most important element, led by reactionary Unionist peers who voted against the Parliament Act of 1911 and the 'Round Table' group of 'Milnerites'. Calling for a programme of national efficiency and imperial protection, the Diehards played a prominent part in driving Balfour from the leadership of the Unionist Party in 1911, and took the lead in exposing the Marconi scandal of 1911–12. They were strongly supported by some elements in the press, especially Leo Maxe's *National Review*. Searle argues the 'radical right' were a force to be reckoned with in Edwardian politics. But they remained deeply split over tactics and lacked a unified leadership or agreed direction, consequently they never offered a coherent alternative to the dominant liberal ethos of their age (Searle, 1979, p. 85; Thurlow, 1987, pp. 2–3).

The Diehards were much more than a declining agrarian elite reacting against modernity. They saw themselves opposing an 'all pervading liberal consensus' operating at the level of Edwardian high politics. Among other things they supported tariff reform, compulsory military service, expansion of the armed services, armed resistance to Home Rule for Ireland and an end to 'alien immigration'. While admiring German efficiency, they were fearful of growing German military and industrial power. Many longed for the *realpolitik* of Bismarckian nationalism and state interventionism (Philips, 1977, pp. 105–20; Thurlow, 1987, pp. 10–11). In effect they were in open revolt against the traditional 'high politics' inherited from the Victorian era. Indeed, 'Victorian' was already a pejorative term for them. Their influence, such as it was, survived through direct links with the British Fascists (BF) in the 1920s, in particular through the efforts of the Eighth Duke of Northumberland who inherited Diehard beliefs from his father and published them and more extreme prejudices in his newspaper *The Patriot* from 1922 onwards.

Much Edwardian 'radical right' activity operating outside the Diehards was centred on defending the Empire from rival imperialist aggression – particularly from Germany. The 'National Service League' agitated for universal conscription. The 'Tariff Reform League', formed in 1903 by Joseph Chamberlain, also attracted radical right adherents with its attacks on *laissez faire* and free trade economic liberalism.

Anti-Semitism was also present in the Edwardian age. The 'British Brothers League', a shadowy organization, orchestrated an 'anti-alien' campaign aimed specifically against Jewish immigration between 1901 and 1906 in alliance with the 'Parliamentary Alien Immigration Committee', the 'London League' and the 'Immigration Reform Association'. Anti-Semitism also surfaced in the campaign waged in 1911–12 by the Chesterton brothers and others in the so-called 'Marconi scandal'. As Thurlow points out this curious mixture of 'jingoism, ethnocentric and conspiratorial anti-Semitism and British imperialism of Edwardian Britain, was a crucial precursor of later British fascism' (Thurlow, 1987, pp. 14–20; Holmes, 1979, p. 91; Fest, 1981, pp. 171–89).

The outbreak of war in 1914 briefly diverted the attention of the radical right, but both Searle and Koss have suggested that the radical right were at least as active and influential during the First World War (Koss, 1969, chs 5–6; Searle, 1979, p. 96). The opening months of the First World War saw renewed radical right criticism of the Liberal government of Asquith, alleging that a 'hidden hand' was burrowing away at the heart of government seeking to betray the national interest to Germany. In the wake of the Bolshevik Revolution in 1917 a plethora of short-lived pressure groups and popular movements grew up to oppose communism and defend the Empire. These included the 'British Empire Union' and the 'National Citizens Union'. The 'National Party' was a classic example of the marginalization of such groups. Founded in 1917 by ex-tariff reformers to attack the coalition government, and calling for the raising of the conscription age to 50, internment of 'enemy aliens, confiscation of German businesses and protection for British industry', the party rejoined the post-war coalition in 1921 to work once again as a faction within the Conservative Party (Thurlow, 1987, pp. 47–9).

THE POST-WAR RADICAL RIGHT AND THE BIRTH OF BRITISH FASCISM

British fascism's first impetus lay in an ultra-conservative response to the social consequences of the First World War and the rise of Bolshevism. The war was clearly of particular importance to the origins of British fascism, representing as it did a radical and urgent right-wing reaction to the continuing decline of imperial Britain, now faced with long-term economic and social problems which had been accelerated and revealed by the war. The radical right (and left) received an injection of ex-soldiers determined to make a better world free from the 'old gangs' of orthodox politicians. Mandle estimated 60 per cent of the fascist elite had been members of the armed forces, while over 40 per cent had seen active service in the First World War (Mandle, 1966, pp. 362–80; Baker, 1982, pp. 39–72). The Bolshevik Revolution traumatized those who already held anti-Semitic and anti-capitalist conspiracy theories, fears further aroused by the appearance throughout Europe of the (forged) Protocols of the Elders of Zion in 1921 (Cohen, 1967, pp. 169–70; Holmes, 1979, pp. 49–85; *idem*, 1977, pp. 13–20; Lebzelter, 1979, pp. 49–85; Blume, 1971, pp. 248–50).

Initial post-war industrial unrest further heightened their paranoia and gave rise to a number of middle-class and imperial defence 'Unions'. Most of the radical right groups that proliferated after the war failed to sustain their impetus. The 'Middle Class Union' (1919) slumped in 1921, briefly reviving in 1926 as the 'National Citizens Union'. The 'Liberty Union' and the more sinister 'National Propaganda' were also short lived and ineffective, and the 'Anti-Socialist and Anti-Communist Union' was similarly marginalized by the strength of the Conservative Party (Summers, 1981, pp. 68–87). The post-war era also witnessed the rise of a new group of 'Diehards', an unofficial parliamentary group who admired their pre-war aristocratic forebears and campaigned for 'true conservatism' against 'Bolshevist Labour Socialism'. Thurlow accurately sums them up as 'an unarmed paramilitary group . . . a cross between an adult boy scout movement and a slightly more sinister defence force and strike breaking organisation' (Thurlow, 1987, p. 24).

The radical right also contained a second and more sinister strand centred on the 'Britons Society' founded in 1918. This group combined conspiratorial anti-Semitism and racist anti-Semitic abuse. Formed by Henry Hamilton Beamish in 1918 (son of an admiral, brother of a Conservative MP, and a soldier in the Boer War) as a 'patriotic' organization dedicated to the eradication of 'alien' influences from British life, the Britons were unique among middle-class defence groups of this period because of their obsessional anti-Semitism. After 1922, they began to disseminate anti-Semitic literature through the 'The Britons Publishing Company'. Beamish also published an anti-Semitic views sheet variously titled *Jewry Uber Alles*, the *Hidden Hand* and the *British Guardian*. The publishing company outlasted its parent by decades publishing 85 editions of 'The Protocols'. Thurlow aptly describes Beamish in his later years (he died in 1948) as a 'kind of travelling salesman of international anti-Semitism' (Thurlow, 1987, pp. 66–8; Lebzelter, 1980, pp. 41–56). As a political ginger group the Britons remained highly marginalized, both by the eccentricity of their views and by the secrecy under which they often operated, remaining 'a small lecturing and debating society with a minuscule middle class membership' (Arronsfield, 1966, pp. 31–5). The chief

The Extreme Right in the 1920s

significance of the organization stemmed from its publishing activities.

The Britons were part of the self-styled 'Jew Wise' group which later included the Imperial Fascist League and the Nordic League, aided by the Duke of Northumberland who published their anti-Semitic outpourings and fantasies in his *Morning Post* and weekly news-sheet *The Patriot*. Virulently anti-Semitic, these groups mixed racial and cultural anti-Semitism with a conspiracy theory, largely based on the 'Protocols'. Contemporary intelligence reports reveal that they were all 'shoestring operations with minimal popular support . . . very few knew of their existence' (Thurlow, 1987, pp. 63–4).

At first sight, the 'British Fascists' (BF) created in 1923 as the British Fascisti and renamed in 1924, appears, in name at least, to be truly fascist. Its founder Rotha Lintorn Orman hailed from a military and girl guide background. She served in an ambulance unit in central Europe in the First World War, and later became Commandant of the national Red Cross Motor School (Griffiths, 1983, pp. 85–93). The BF's activities centred on military style discipline, organized strike-breaking and stewarding right-wing Conservative meetings. But they were little more than another disaffected middle-class defence league, made up largely of Conservatives obsessed with the dangers of civil strife and Bolshevism, and seeking to maintain public order and guarantee essential services through a network of paramilitary units if Red Revolution should come to the Home Counties. It actually urged its supporters to vote for the Conservative party during elections. Scholars agree that it did little more than borrow the name from Italy, never attracting more than a handful of well-to-do supporters, with a membership mainly comprised of military, naval and 'county' types, 'with the lower orders consisting of loyal working class toughs' (Griffiths, 1983, pp. 85–7; Blakeney, 1925; Benewick, 1971, pp. 28–9; Thurlow, 1987, pp. 60–1).

The leadership were unable to agree on the role the organization should play during the General Strike. Their offer to help the Organization for the Maintenance of Supplies (OMS) was refused unless they dismantled their military organization and dropped the term 'fascist'. Faced with a refusal several prominent members resigned and formed the 'Loyalists' which was allowed by the government to assist the OMS (Griffiths, 1983, p. 88). The movement, deeply divided within three years of its creation, finally collapsed in a moribund state in 1935 (Griffiths, 1983, p. 163).

The BF was in no way anti-capitalist nor (officially at least) anti-Semitic (Griffiths, 1983, p. 88). As Benewick has argued their influence was negligible and they were largely ignored: 'Political forces on neither the right nor the left took them seriously' (Benewick, 1971, p. 38). Griffiths concluded that it never escaped its early image as a 'glorified Boys' Brigade run by women'. Gerry Webber also stresses its relative unimportance both ideologically and organizationally. He characterizes the BF as dominated by the upper-middle or middle classes, and minor aristocrats, still influenced by the inter-war Conservative party (Griffiths, 1983, p. 96; Webber, 1987, pp. 28–9).

Recently, Lunn has sought to revise our picture of the BF as a largely middle-class ginger group. He claims that 'the BF have been undervalued by existing studies, in the sense both of their contribution to later fascist groups and ideology, and in an assessment of their significance in a crucial formative period of British politics, the 1920s.' He further claims that 'the range of branch activity in the 1920s was impressive,' suggesting: 'It would also be a mistake to see the members of the organisation as wholly middle or upper-middle-class.' He points out that: 'The Army Council issued an order in 1925 that all men were prohibited from joining the BF . . . indicating concern in the military authorities . . .' and that the 'extent of working class support has also been neglected, with the exception of Griffiths and Thurlow's passing comments . . . collectively, the weight of examples suggests the need for a revision of the "middle class" label . . . in order to play down its significance as a genuine mass movement, one of the crucial indicators of fascist organisation.' Finally, Lunn shows evidence of 'blatant and highly public encapsulation of a Jewish conspiracy theory . . . By 1928 . . . the policy on "Aliens" was made clear: "NB Jews are in all cases mentioned, regarded as Aliens"' (Lunn, 1989, pp. 140–54).

But Thurlow's assessment remains the more convincing:

> The organization lacked coherent leadership and purpose and was little more than a patriotic group with a foreign sounding name . . . it had no leadership cult . . . Its importance for the development of fascism in Britain has to be

seen in terms of the administration and discipline ... BF policy was vague and generalised. Its main components included the upholding of the monarchy, promotion of class friendship, the elimination of slums, the encouragement of Empire trade, a drastic restriction of immigration and deep seated hostility to socialism and Bolshevism. There was no overt anti-Semitism before 1932.
(Thurlow, 1987, pp. 57–61)

Nevertheless the BF did provide a training ground for several members of the fascist movement of the 1930s, with Arnold Leese, William Joyce and Neil Francis Hawkins all members at one time or another. It also became increasingly anti-Semitic and 'fascist' in its death throes in 1933–4, disappearing after Orman's early death in 1935. Some of the more aggressive anti-Semites, realizing their mistake, had split off from the BF to form the British National Fascisti as early as 1925. Arnold Leese remarked famously that '... there was no Fascism, as I understood it, in the organisation, which was merely Conservatism with Knobs On ...' (Leese, 1951, p. 49). Leese also left in disgust and founded the 'Imperial Fascist League' in 1929. It represented the nearest approximation to a fascist organization in 1920s Britain, being virulently anti-Semitic and fervently pro-Nazi in character. Leese, a vet (and a leading expert on camel diseases), was elected on a British Fascist programme to Stamford council in 1924. He was decisively influenced by Arthur Kitson of the 'Britons'. Kitson, the currency reformer and a close neighbour of Leese in Stamford, convinced him that the Jewish money power was behind all the evil in the world.

The IFL had pretentions to be a 'true' fascist movement. Its journal *The Fascist* saw fascism as a collectivist and pan-European ideal. A corporate state was proposed ruled ultimately by a 'Fascist Grand Council', currency would be reformed and Jews would 'lose their citizenship ...' As Thurlow puts it: 'Jewish Money-Power' was their enemy and 'The Protocols of the Elders of Zion their Bible' (Thurlow, 1984, p. 98). But judged as a political party the IFL was, like all the other radical right and proto-fascist groups in Britain in the 1920s, of highly marginal political significance. Its main 'achievement' was to provide yet another training organization for eccentric anti-Semitic and anti-Bolshevik propagandists.

FAILED OR MARGINALIZED?

> One should not exaggerate the importance of the radical right during this period, nor its cohesion. Its influence was always confined to a relatively small fringe of argumentative political activists, most of whom were supporters, and many of whom were members of the Conservative Party . . . and by 1926 they were in almost total disarray . . .
> (Webber, in Kushner and Lunn, 1989, pp. 156–7)

If nothing else emerges from the discussion above, it is that British fascist movements in the 1920s had fundamental and fatal weaknesses in terms of their elites, organizations and ideologies. The intertwining of virulent political anti-Semitism with Diehard reactionary conservatism characterized the bulk of 1920s so-called 'fascist' activity in Britain. A large number of these 'precursors' of British fascism appeared more interested in anti-revolutionary propaganda than political power – the driving force behind Nazi success in Germany – and never fully emancipated themselves from the Conservative Party (Benewick, 1971, p. 23; Webber, 1989, pp. 154–72).

Their real problem, as Webber points out, 'was in finding a message that worked politically.' Nationalism, patriotism, militarism, anti-alienism, anti-socialism, all highly successful forms of propaganda in Germany, failed to add up to a political ideology of sufficient power to undermine British Conservative Party propaganda, or to make Labour appear as a threat to freedom. Equally, attacks on Parliamentary democracy so shortly after the successful extension of the franchise and a celebrated victory over the Germans was never a realistic proposition. Nor was there constitutional paralysis in Britain akin to that of Italy in 1922 where no one could be found to form a government, or that of Weimar Germany with *Reich* Chancellors only able to rule by emergency decree.

Webber has usefully enumerated a number of long-term factors which inhibited growth of the radical and fascist right in Britain. These include: the lack of any foreign invasions since the eleventh century; a unified nation state since the eighteenth century; a relatively peaceful transition to parliamentary democracy under existing landed and bourgeois elites; a strong sense of national identity; the lack of mass immigrations or migrations on the scale seen in central Europe; victory in the

First World War; a relatively short post-war recession and no hyperinflation; a powerful Conservative Party at ease with mass democracy; a highly reformist social democratic Labour opposition linked to the Lib-Lab traditions of the Victorian age; a trade union movement largely free from syndicalist tendencies; few social groups sufficiently alienated from the dominant political culture; and a relatively weak tradition of revolutionary Communism (Webber, 1989, pp. 168–9).

Consequently, relatively few members of the middle classes in Britain were afraid that Bolshevism would rapidly spread to the end of the Northern Line, or that the Labour Party was simply a Trojan horse for the Bolshevik's imminent takeover. Crucially, unlike in Germany and Russia, the war had enjoyed at least the tacit consent of most of the home population. Britain emerged from the war victorious, and there was no appreciable post-war 'fiscal crisis of the state' and considerably less economic dislocation in Britain than in Italy or Germany. German prices peaked at one million million times the 1914 levels in 1923, wiping out middle-class savings and leaving many threatened with eviction from their homes and even starvation. Bitter memories of this humiliation lingered on to dog the Weimar politicians. In Britain the cost of living index trend fell from 1922 to 1933. Thus, radical rightist parties seeking to utilize middle-class discontent were given an easy task in Germany by comparison with Britain (Mitchell, 1975, pp. 739 and 746; Aldcroft, 1977, p. 15).

In addition, while there is a native British tradition of intolerance and authoritarianism, it has remained a relatively unimportant feature of British politics, leading to the marginalization of the 'Jew Wise' radical right in the 1920s. The agricultural revolutions of the eighteenth and nineteenth centuries, coupled with changes wrought by the 'Great Depression', had removed the British peasantry – a group highly receptive to anti-Semitic, anti-modernist ideas throughout mainland Europe. Equally, there was no equivalent to the German *Deutschnationaler Handlungshilfenverband* to represent lower middle-class prejudices. British landed elites were on the whole comfortable with industrial capitalism, unlike their Prussian *Junker* counterparts.

This was reflected in the pragmatism of the British Conservatives. Disraeli had turned the Tory Party from the party of aristocratic privilege and reaction into a modern mass-based party, willing to allow social and political reform, and 'permitting' political participation by Labour's representatives, at least to those willing to adhere to the parliamentary rules. The Liberal Party had long accepted this arrangement with Labour. By way of contrast, in Germany the Social Democrats and trade unions were treated with the utmost suspicion by the German establishment. Germany's ruling elites obstinately faced down a popular and powerful workers' party which actively questioned the legitimacy of the existing order. They also faced a powerful Catholic centre party, holding the balance between left and right in the *Reichstag*, at the cost of paralysing the parliamentary system. In Britain, industrial militancy died away in the early 1920s, and the left was dominated by a moderate, parliamentary Labour Party, welcomed by some Conservatives as part of the official opposition in order to split the anti-Conservative vote (Cowling, 1971).

The popular appeal of the Conservative Party was a key factor in marginalizing the early fascists. Baldwin's modernized Conservative party studiously ignored these groups, and the electorate continued to respond to the cautious consensus politics of the Conservative and Labour Parties. The British political structure withstood the strain of economic dislocation and industrial unrest with the old order still largely intact, and able to outface the General Strike of 1926 (Stephenson, 1990, p. 268).

Stevenson, rightly, sees this as a crucial factor:

> Ultimately, the failure of the BUF and of the earlier fascist movements to gain greater support must be attributed to the established parties' success during the interwar years in maintaining and even increasing their support... fears of Bolshevism and economic ruin... served to maintain and increase support for the Conservative Party... offering a safe bulwark to property and order... Britain's strong Conservative Party virtually monopolised the ground on which any fascist movement might hope to base itself...
> (Stevenson, 1990, pp. 275–6)

Indeed, during the 1920s there was little opportunity for extremist parties to gain any purchase on the left either. Founded in 1921, the 'Communist Party of Great Britain' (CPGB) remained dwarfed by the Labour Party, the trade union movement and even working-class Toryism (Stevenson, 1990, p. 268).

Anti-socialism also made little headway outside the Conservative Party, with a highly reformist and moderate, not to say orthodox, Labour Party dominating the left (Gamble, 1990, pp. 92–3).

In addition, Britain was a well-established nation state even before the advent of industrialization, while the German Empire was a recent foundation and whose shape and form remained uncertain. This gave rise to an exaggerated patriotism and nationalism in Germany. There was no widespread feeling of impending national or imperial disaster in Britain; if anything there was a rather complacent sense of national superiority amongst most of the population (Kennedy and Nicholls, 1981, pp. 14–16). Militarism in Britain (a crucial factor in the rise of German Nazism) was much less popular in inter-war Britain, a fact made clear from the history of the ex-serviceman's movement (Webber, 1989, p. 160).

Anti-alienism appeared to offer richer ideological soil. Yet it too proved incapable of sustaining any independent mass movements of significance. As Webber has pointed out, much of the anti-Semitic propaganda of the 1920s was 'aimed at middle class worries about industrial unrest and aristocratic anxieties about industrial development, rather than working class fears about immigration' (Webber, 1987, p. 59). British fascism could only rely upon residual upper-class 'golf-club' anti-Semitism and anti-Jewish feeling in some working-class areas, notably London's East End, but elsewhere it put off far more people than it attracted. As Thurlow has stated: 'The fact that Britain had neither a co-ordinated integral nationalist populist movement, nor was influenced significantly by romantic nationalism before 1914 helps to explain the uphill task which British fascists faced in their later attempts to revolutionise society' (Thurlow, 1987, pp. 20–1).

Thus, early British fascism had to operate in a politically, economically and culturally cold climate. The British economy was never subjected to the full force of international recession, protected as it was by its albeit declining Empire, even in 1929 (Gamble, 1990, p. 137). Labour unrest seldom threatened to destabilize the political system and when it did, in 1926, the threat was quickly and effectively neutralized by clever state management of the situation by the Conservative government. The vast majority of the electorate maintained their belief in the parliamentary system. There was no equivalent to the deep-rooted *völkisch* nationalism and chauvinism of German political culture. Clear evidence of this can be seen from the fact that most of those who called themselves 'fascists' in the 1920s were really preaching what Leese called 'Conservatism with Knobs on'. Reciprocal hostility between the so-called fascists and the Left was also a considerable problem for them, since this led to violent confrontations which further damaged their image as upholders of 'law and order'. Ironically, for groups constantly attacking the 'alien' forces in society, fascism itself appeared as a foreign import to potential converts to the creed – hence the change in the title of the British Fascisti to the British Fascists in 1924.

Taken together, and combined with the obvious eccentricity of fascist ideas and personnel, such factors caused British fascism to be effectively marginalized from its very inception. 'Marginalization' rather than 'failure' is a more accurate term for this process, since failure implies that there was a prospect of success in 1920s Britain. In fact, given the 'cold climate' of socio-economic, political and historical forces ranged against it, the various groups claiming to represent British fascism were all trapped in a political ghetto from the very outset. It is difficult to envisage any tactics, organization or propaganda which could have released them from this, without the prior occurrence of a considerable deterioration in the socioeconomic and/or political contexts of the period. Proof of this can be found in the fact that even Mosley's truly 'fascist' movement, with its superior funding, publicity and organization, could not overcome the problems of marginalization in the depression years of the 1930s.

REFERENCES

Aldcroft, D.H., *From Versailles to Wall Street, 1919–1929* (Harmondsworth, 1977).

Arronsfield, C.C., *The Britons Publishing Society*, Weiner Library Bulletin, No. 20, Summer 1966, pp. 31–5.

Baker, D.L., 'The making of a British Fascist: The case of A.K. Chesterton, PhD thesis, Sheffield University, 1982.

Benewick, R.J., *The Fascist Movement in Britain* (London, 1971).
Biddiss, M.D., *The Age of the Masses* (Harmondsworth, 1977).
Blakeney, R., *British Fascism, Nineteenth Century and After* (London, 1925).
Blinkhorn, M. (ed.), *Fascists and Conservatives* (London, 1990).
Blume, H., 'A history of anti-Semitic groups 1918–1940', unpublished MPhil thesis, University of Sussex, 1971.
Cohen, N., *Warrant for Genocide* (London, 1967).
Cole, J.A., *Lord Haw Haw – and William Joyce: The Full Story* (London, 1964).
Cowling, M., *The Impact of Labour, 1920–24* (Cambridge, 1971).
Dangerfield, G., *The Strange Death of Liberal England* (London, 1970).
Fest, W., 'Jingoism and xenophobia in the electioneering strategies of British ruling elites before 1914', in Kennedy, P. and Nicholls, A. (eds), *Nationalist and Racialist Movements in Britain before 1914* (Oxford, 1981).
Gamble, A., *Britain in Decline* (Basingstoke, 1990).
Griffiths, R., *Fellow Travellers of the Right: British Enthusiasts for Nazi Germany 1933–1939* (Oxford, 1983).
Holmes, C., 'New light on the "Protocols of Zion"', *Patterns of Prejudice*, November–December, 1977.
Holmes, C., *Anti-Semitism in British Society 1876–1939* (London, 1979).
Hope, J., 'Fascism and the state in Britain: the case of the British Fascisti 1923–31', *Australian Journal of Politics and History*, Vol. 39, No. 3, 1993, pp. 367–80.
Kennedy, P., 'The pre-war right in Britain and Germany', in Kennedy, P. and Nicholls, A. (eds), *Nationalist and Racialist Movements in Britain before 1914* (Oxford, 1981).
Kennedy, P. and Nicholls, A., *Nationalist and Racialist Movements in Britain and Germany before 1914* (Oxford, 1981).
Koss, S.E., *Lord Haldane: Scapegoat for Liberalism* (London, 1969).
Kushner, T. and Lunn, K., *Traditions of Intolerance: Historical Perspectives on Fascism and Race Discourse in Britain* (Manchester, 1989).
Lebzelter, G., *Political Anti-Semitism in England 1918–1939* (London, 1979).
Lebzelter, G., 'Henry Hamilton Beamish and the Britons. Champions of anti-Semitism', in Lunn, K. and Thurlow, R.C. (eds), *British Fascism* (London, 1980).
Leese, A., *Out of Step: Events in the Two Lives of an Anti-Jewish Camel Doctor* (Guildford, 1951).
Lunn, K, 'Political anti-Semitism before 1914: Fascism's heritage', in Lunn, K. and Thurlow, R.C. (eds), *British Fascism* (London, 1980), pp. 20–40.
Lunn, K., 'The ideology and impact of the British Fascists in the 1920s', in Kushner, T. and Lunn, K. (eds), *Traditions of Intolerance: Historical Perspectives on Fascism and Race Discourse in Britain* (Manchester, 1989), pp. 140–54.
Mandle, W.F., 'The leadership of the British Union of Fascists', *Australian Journal of Politics and History*, December 1966, pp. 362–80.
Marsden, V. (trans.), *Protocols of the Learned Elders of Zion* (London, 1920).
Mitchell, B.R., *European Historical Statistics: 1750–1970* (London, 1975).
Morell, J., 'The life and times of A.S. Leese. A study in extreme anti-Semitism', MA thesis, University of Sheffield, 1974.
Morell, J., 'Arnold Leese and the Imperial Fascist League: the impact of racial fascism', in Lunn, K. and Thurlow, R.C. (eds), *British Fascism* (London, 1980), pp. 57–76.

Philips, G.D., 'The Die-hards and the myth of the backwoodsmen', *Journal of British Studies*, Vol. 16, Spring 1977.

Rubinstein, W.D., 'Henry Page Croft and the National Party, 1918–1922', *Journal of Contemporary History*, 1974, Vol. 9, No. 1, pp. 129–48.

Searle, G., 'Critics of Edwardian society: the case of the radical right', in O'Day, A. (ed.), *The Edwardian Age* (London, 1979).

Searle, G., 'The revolt from the right in Edwardian Britain', in Kennedy, P. and Nicholls, A. (eds), *Nationalist and Racialist Movements in Britain before 1914* (Oxford, 1981).

Stevenson, J., 'Conservatism and the failure of fascism in interwar Britain', in Blinkhorn, M. (ed.), *Fascists and Conservatives* (London, 1990).

Summers, A., 'The character of Edwardian nationalism: three popular Leagues', in Kennedy, P. and Nicholls, A. (eds), *Nationalist and Racialist Movements in Britain before 1914* (Oxford, 1981).

Thorpe, A. (ed.), *The Failure of Political Extremism in Inter-War Britain*, Exeter Studies in History No. 21, Exeter University, 1989.

Thurlow, R.C., *Fascism in Britain: A History 1918–85* (Oxford, 1987).

Thurlow, R.C., 'The failure of British Fascism – 1932–40', in Thorpe, A. (ed.), *The Failure of Political Extremism in Inter-War Britain*, Exeter Studies in History No. 21, Exeter University, 1989.

Thurlow, R.C., *The Secret State: British Internal Security in the Twentieth Century* (Oxford, 1995).

Webber, G.C., 'Intolerance and discretion: Conservatives and British Fascism', in Kushner, T. and Lunn, K. (eds), *Traditions of Intolerance: Historical Perspectives on Fascism and Race Discourse in Britain* (Manchester, 1989), pp. 155–72.

Webber, G.C., *The Ideology of the British Right, 1918–39* (London, 1987).

NOTE

1. I have adopted Roger Griffin's typology in the use of fascism with a small or capital 'f'. Thus, 'fascism' with a small 'f' denotes the generic form of fascism, while spelt with a large 'F' Fascism denotes the specific Italian variant. See R. Griffin, *The Nature of Fascism* (London, 1991), p. 185 *passim*.

3 State Management of the British Union of Fascists in the 1930s
Richard Thurlow

One of the more intriguing aspects of the state management of political extremism in twentieth-century Britain has been the attitude of the authorities towards British fascism. We know more about the political surveillance of the British Union of Fascist (BUF) than any other movement which was of concern to government in the inter-war period, as a result of four releases of Home Office files on the subject between 1983 and 1986. In 1995 more material was declassified, including documents on the traitors William Joyce and John Amery. While it is quite clear that official views across the entire range of levels of state activity towards British fascism have been uniformly hostile, there is now some evidence emerging that certain elements within the secret state had a more ambiguous interpretation of the phenomenon.

The role of the state in the failure of British fascism in the inter-war period can now be assessed as a consequence of such material. Before the state management of the BUF is examined, however, it is necessary to look briefly at two related issues: the anti-communist phobia between 1918 and 1939, and the attitude of the authorities towards the first British fascist organization, the British Fascisti (renamed the British Fascists in 1924 – BF). This is of relevance both with regard to the comparison of state management of extremist groups, and the secrecy still surrounding the release of documents on both organizations.

While there is no doubt that the Communist Party of Great Britain (CPGB) represented the main object of political surveillance in the United Kingdom by the authorities in the inter-war period, the documentation does not reflect this fact after 1924. It was then that Special Branch became concerned about the security of the fortnightly reports on revolutionary activities in Great Britain, following the creation of the first Labour government in January 1924. After an exchange of letters between the new Prime Minister, Ramsay Macdonald, and the head of Special Branch, Sir Wyndham Childs, the Cabinet no longer received these sometimes lurid, and often inaccurate, documents as a matter of routine. This, however, does not alter the fact that the mindset of the security authorities, particularly MI5, MI6 and Special Branch, egged on by the military, the Metropolitan Police Commissioners, the right wing of the Conservative Party, and some Labour Party politicians, continued to be obsessed with the alleged conspiracy, hatched in Moscow Centre. Such a view took seriously the unrealistic proposition that the CPGB would lead the British masses to revolutionary activity.

This fear coexisted with the British political reality of economic weakness, retrenchment and massive cuts in public expenditure after the First World War. Like today, this affected the military, police and security authorities, as much as social and welfare reforms. Although MI5 and Special Branch, unlike the Directorate of Intelligence, were to survive the drastic security pruning operation, they were to do so on a very much reduced scale, compared with the proliferation of political surveillance during the First World War. Paranoia and parsimony were to coexist in harmony, and this was to be reflected in the nature of political snooping.

John Hope has shown how the security authorities used the sometimes inaccurate political intelligence of reputable middle-class organizations, like the British Empire Union, the National Citizens Union, the Anti-Socialist Union, the National Security Union, the Liberty League and the Economic League, through the coordinating role of National Propaganda, to provide much of the information for the Directorate of Intelligence, between 1919 and 1921, and as an input to Special Branch after that date. This, apparently, was not the least of the ex-Director of Naval Intelligence, Sir Reginald 'Blinker' Hall's many contributions to Britain's secret history between 1914 and 1926. The discovery that Maxwell Knight, the Intelligence Officer of the BF, was also an MI5 agent from 1925, fits into the same pattern, as he was a member of the British Empire Union (Hope, 1992, p. 74; Hope, 1993, pp. 367–80; Hope, 1994, pp. 651–75). Not only did MI5 recruit directly from patriotic organizations, but this was a cheap way of cutting costs in financing political surveillance. Incidentally, this connection shows that MI5 had already strayed beyond its brief in investigating communist influence in the British armed forces, and had already, before the 1931 creation of the security service, become actively involved in civilian surveillance (Hinsley and Simkins, 1990, p. 9). That Knight's connection was not an isolated case can be shown by the fact that other intelligence agents were also recruited, or were infiltrated, into the BF (Thurlow, 1994, pp. 203–13).

This intelligence interest in the BF has to be contrasted with the view from Whitehall. The official image of the BF was that it was a disreputable and irresponsible organization. A Foreign Office minute stated that in Britain they were treated with 'derision or contempt'. (PRO FO 371/11384/C9108). The Home Office file on the BF portrayed them as a highly eccentric organization, surviving on the resources of its founder, Rotha Lintorn Orman, who during the 1920s was allegedly dependent on alcohol and drugs. Such an anti-feminist and anti-suffragette bias displayed a disparaging tone against women in politics. Sir William Joynson-Hicks (Jix), the right-wing Home Secretary in 1926, threatened to resign as Vice President of the National Citizens Union if the BF were allowed to help the authorities in the Organization for the Maintenance of Supplies. This attitude has to be contrasted with the fact that the BF appeared to be honeycombed with intelligence agents. The explanation of this Janus-faced attitude towards the organization derived from the need-to-know principle. Politicians and civil servants saw the BF purely as a public order nuisance, whose existence provoked the left. MI5, on the other hand, saw it as a possible ally against the 'red menace'. This could assist the authorities with voluntary help in an emergency, and through its links with the surviving private middle-class intelligence networks, had surveillance in place which could provide cheap information about revolutionary threats. The secrecy of MI5, and the lack of operational oversight of the organization, meant the machinery of government had little idea of the nature of the details of how British security was administered in the 1930s.

The official contemptuous dismissal of British fascism altered when Sir Oswald Mosley became a fascist in 1932, particularly with relation to the connections between the BUF and the

Italian Fascists and German Nazis, and the increased public order problems arising from clashes between the BUF and the CPGB in 1933. The view of British fascism in Whitehall in the 1930s was almost uniformly a negative one, although there was concern about sympathy for fascism in some sections of the establishment, particularly with the views of the Prince of Wales, who became Edward VIII in 1936. This interest concerned Mosley's personal, social and economic connections with the aristocracy, big business and the armed services, and the apparently unconnected activities of the German embassy and Nazi agents in London.

In particular, the activities of the January Club, a social and dining club, which enabled the BUF to discuss its case with right-wing members of the establishment in a convivial environment, were of particular concern to the authorities. This organization wined and dined an interesting cross section of Conservative MPs, the landed aristocracy, military officers and entrepreneurs in the 1930s. These meetings attracted several hundred participants in 1934. The released MI5 reports on the BUF concentrate on providing material about the connections with the fascist powers, links with the establishment and armed forces, public order concerns and the nature of the membership and its spatial distribution. The information seeping upwards from the secret state about British fascism strengthened the hostility felt towards the personality of Sir Oswald Mosley within high politics in the inter-war period.

Although some right-wing Conservatives, including for a time Winston Churchill, admired Mussolini for his firm stand against social unrest and communism in Italy, only a few Tory mavericks, like A.H. Maule Ramsay, Michael Beaumont and Lt. Colonel T.C.R. Moore, were to excuse the BUF behaviour in Parliament. Most supporters of the National government agreed with Baldwin, that 'Tom Mosley was a cad and a wrong 'un' (Jones, 1969, p. 195). They objected to both his political cavortings and his personal lifestyle which so offended the narrow nonconformist conscience that dominated the politics of the inter-war period. Most Conservative opinion at the Olympia meeting on 7 June 1934 blamed Mosley for the violence, and thought he had been deliberately provocative in ejecting interrupters rather than trying to answer them (290 HC Deb 5s, 11 June 1934, 1935–7, 1952–3).

Both the Labour and Liberal parties were hostile to what they perceived as the authoritian and elitist structure of the BUF. They objected to fascist stewards at meetings and the paramilitary aspects of Mosley's Blackshirts. Labour politicians considered Mosley a traitor; Dalton called fascists a 'political bad smell' (317 HC Deb 5s, 5 November 1936, 294–7), and Attlee thought Mosley was a megalomaniac who was not entirely stable (309 HC Deb 5s, 27 February 1936, 294–7). Morrison argued, in the aftermath of Cable Street, that all the political parties in the East End of London wanted the fascists banned (PRO HO 144/21062/10–45). Political pressures also came from trade unions. The Amalgamated Society of Locomotive Engineers and Firemen complained of BUF plans for the suppression of Parliament, the imprisonment of opponents and the establishment of a private army (PRO HO 144/20140/7–8). Labour argued that unless the government took action against the BUF, the party would be unable to control the justified anger of extremists, who were already forming anti-fascist organizations such as the Greyshirts (PRO HO 144/20141/51).

That such public hostility to the BUF should be expressed by representatives of the 'old gangs' of British politics was not surprising, given that Mosley's aim was to replace parliamentary government with the corporate state, and to outlaw all political opposition parties to the BUF. Such negative views, however, expressed from all sides of the House of Commons, did not make the administrative problems of regulating fascist activity and the imposition of legal restraints any easier.

The preferred method for dealing with British fascism was through informal techniques of political management. Tinkering with the common law was viewed as a measure of last resort by the politicians and the Home Office, as it let out a Pandora's box of problems, which included resistance to the restrictions on civil liberties, a dread of special legislation discriminating against, or about, specific groups, and limited the administrative freedom of manoeuvre and discretion by the authorities. Hence pressure was applied to the media, either in the form of polite requests from the government, or in more subtle ways, to secure the cooperation of Sir John Reith at the BBC. After the ending of Rothermere's 'Hurrah for the Blackshirts' campaign in the *Daily Mail* in July 1934, it appeared that the National government approached newspaper editors and asked them to avoid unnecessary publicity for the BUF. The BBC avoided presentation of extremist views through an unofficial ban which denied fascists and communists, as well as independent maverick opinion critical of government policy, including Winston Churchill, in the 1930s. Indeed Mosley, as well as CPGB speakers, was not allowed to broadcast until 1968. Finally newsreel companies were asked not to film mass demonstrations in the 1930s (PRO HO 144/20710/3; MEPO 2/5507; West, 1987, p. 91). Only when such measures were shown to be insufficient in 1936 was the nettle finally grasped, and the politicians strengthened the powers necessary to maintain public order.

The problem of the regulation of public order in the 1930s has proved one of the most controversial aspects of state management of fascism in the inter-war period. Recent interpretations of the Public Order Act of 1936 have tended to place the fascist disturbances of the 1930s in a wider context. This has seen changes in the law as primarily a response to left-wing mass demonstrations in the inter-war period, particularly to the issues raised by unemployment marches, militant trade unionism and communist activities (Anderson, 1983; Lewis, 1987, pp. 145–80; Morgan, 1987, pp. 229–75). The conflict generated between Mosley's Blackshirt's and anti-fascists was merely the trigger mechanism for changes in the law, which had been formulated as a response to previous concerns. D.S. Lewis, echoing the contemporary criticisms of the National Council for Civil Liberties (NCCL) in the 1930s, has gone further, and criticized the 'reactionary' and 'regressive' measures passed by the National government with regard to public order and internal security issues in the 1930s.

While such interpretations have to be borne in mind, it is a mistake to see changes in the law solely as an unnecessary restriction on civil liberty, or as a conscious or unconscious centralization of power. Although the activities of MI5, Special Branch and the uniformed police in the inter-war period obviously heightened the authorities' concern about public order and internal security, there were important countervailing tendencies pulling in the opposite direction. Changes in the law were dependent on political factors, and although the right wing of the Conservative Party and other security conscious

MPs were influenced by such concerns, many politicians viewed the activities of MI5 and Special Branch with scepticism and distaste. The vociferous campaign, with both the opposition's objections to the Incitement to Disaffection Act of 1934 and the low politics marches and protests against it, orchestrated by the CPGB and the NCCL, led to the government becoming very cautious in pushing through legislation with relation to public order and internal security which did not have a parliamentary consensus behind it.

Indeed opposition parties were to hold what was in effect a veto power on much of the content and operation of the Public Order Act after 1936. It was the failure to gain cross party backing for legislation in 1932 and 1934 which accounted for the government abandoning plans to bring in new legislation in those years. Politicians from all the parliamentary parties were reluctant to limit rights of assembly, and only hesitantly moved to change the law when police powers to manage civil disorders were shown to be inadequate as a consequence of the 'Battle of Cable Street' on 4 October 1936.

Within Whitehall there were also important administrative forces which acted to counteract the restrictionist attitude of the security authorities in the 1930s. The permanent officials of the Home Office interpreted the law in a liberal manner, and acted as a conservative brake on over-enthusiastic, or impatient, police and security officers. The Home Office officials were suspicious of the Colonial Office influence and military background of many in the police and security administrations. Always emphasizing the necessity for caution, they stressed the need to have sufficient powers to control and discourage fascist–communist violence, whilst at the same time preserving the maximum degree of civil liberty.

It was the Home Office which was responsible for regulating public order policy, and provided the legal framework through which the authorities managed British fascism. In the 1930s four very different Home Secretaries, Sir John Gilmour (1932–5), Sir John Simon (1935–7), Sir Samuel Hoare (1937–9) and Sir John Anderson (1939–40), reacted according to the conflicting advice they received from the Home Office, the Cabinet, Parliament, the law officers, the Metropolitan Police Commissioners, the chief constables and public opinion. Of these Gilmour and Hoare tended to follow the advice of Lord

Trenchard and Sir Philip Game, their respective Metropolitan Police Commissioners, while Simon, a previous law officer and Home Secretary, was more inclined towards the more liberal advice of his officials, and Anderson, the personification of the traditions of the Home Office, was prepared to challenge the increased authority of MI5 once war had broken out.

The permanent Home Office officials under Sir Russell Scott (1932–8) and Sir Alexander Maxwell (1938–48), as Under-Secretaries of State, played an increasingly important role in upholding the liberal traditions of the Home Office. The continuity of policy and personnel is perhaps best illustrated by the part played by Frank Newsam, deputy to Sir Arthur Dixon in the Police Department, the Home Office mandarin most concerned with law and order and security matters in the 1930s. Newsam was later knighted, and became Permanent Under-Secretary between 1948 and 1958.

The struggle for influence between the authoritarian style of management of Lord Trenchard, as Metropolitan Police Commissioner, and the permanent officials was to be an important ingredient in developing policy. Certainly this conflict was to show that tightening Home Office control over the police, while increasing the discretion of the chief constables, was to be only partly achieved in the inter-war period (Boyle, 1962, pp. 665–8; Morgan, 1987, p. 276). More influence was to be exerted over Sir Philip Game, who was later to moderate the impact of Trenchard's radical police reforms. The Home Office officials did not wish to increase the powers of the Home Secretary, nor to undermine local autonomy. They basically reacted to events, and only suggested changes in the common law as a result of political initiative or the impact of conflict. Even then it was only after painstaking research had been examined. The banning of paramilitary organizations in section 2 of the Public Order Act 1936 was only agreed after a comparative survey of European developments, and it was decided that Swedish legislation would provide the best model for Britain.

The Home Office view was developed in response to pressure applied by the chief constables, particularly the Metropolitan Police Commissioners. Apart from voicing general worries and tendering advice in Circulars that various chief constables and watch committees were exceeding their powers in prohibiting or threatening to ban BUF marches and meetings, the Home Office had little control over police policy outside the metropolis. It was very concerned that over-vigilant policing would be challenged successfully in the courts (PRO HO 144/20158/72; HO 144/20143/107).

This was shown in the administrative response to over-zealous police activity in Leicester and Manchester, prior to the passing of the Public Order Act, as the Home Office mandarins worried about possible infringement by the authorities of freedom of association and expression. In fact the courts were to uphold the legality of police intervention, and extension of powers, even before the passing of the Public Order Act in December 1936.

The problem for the Home Office was further complicated by the personality of the Metropolitan Police Commissioner between 1931 and 1935, Lord Trenchard. Brought in to reform the Metropolitan Police, he had ridden roughshod over some of the objections presented by Home Office officials, and had appealed successfully to Sir John Gilmour over their heads. Although he cooperated fairly amicably with Arthur Dixon, the sometimes fraught relations between Home Office officials and the Metropolitan Police Commissioner found expression in differences in public order policy as well (Trenchard Papers, MFC 76/1/314/25; PRO HO 144/20158/186–87, 350–57). Trenchard considered several leading Home Office officials to be administrative lightweights.

These problems were shown quite clearly in 1934, in response to Trenchard's call for banning the BUF. The Home Office replied that the same consideration still applied as when General Horwood, the Metropolitan Police Commissioner between 1920 and 1928, requested a ban on the CPGB. There was no argument for outlawing extremist beliefs provided the expression of such policies did not break the law. Only if the authorities' management of the situation under existing powers appeared to be threatened could changes in the law be contemplated. So long as public opinion believed we had a fair and efficient government, which upheld the law, the state should not attempt to restrict the holding of political beliefs, no matter how obnoxious they appeared to those who held democratic values. Political surveillance of such movements was necessary, but attempts to restrict liberty would drive political expression underground, and create worse problems in the long run (PRO HO 144/20158/162–63).

Trenchard's trenchant views on fascists were somewhat ironic given that the communists accused him of being a closet fascist himself because of his autocratic style of management and the alleged close connections Mosley had with the RAF, of which the Metropolitan Police Commissioner had been the founder. Trenchard wished to ban the fascists because of the public order problems they presented and the waste of police resources associated with controlling processions and meetings. He particularly wanted to outlaw the wearing of uniforms and paramilitary organizations. He did not want uniformed stewarding of meetings outside police control, neither did he want the police to be seen as protecting fascists. He was also concerned that 'respectable' people would appear on CPGB platforms in support of their anti-fascist activity. The police should also be given powers to enter meetings to prevent disturbance (PRO HO 144/20158/186–87). Just before his retirement he began to advocate the view that fascist processions should be banned.

Trenchard's case developed in response to practical problems after it was made clear to him that restricting the rights of fascists outside the use of emergency powers was not a feasible political or legal option. Trenchard was succeeded as Metropolitan Police Commissioner in 1935 by Sir Philip Game, who as his leading administrator in the RAF had been personally chosen to succeed him. Although the Home Office officials found him more reasonable to deal with, however, he was even more anti-fascist than his predecessor. Game wished to outlaw political anti-Semitism and to ban the fascist movement (PRO HO 144/20159/155–62). His experience as Governor-General of New South Wales in the early 1930s, when he had sacked the Prime Minister and had problems with fascist demonstrations, gave him the right background for dealing with the troubles in the East End (Foott, 1968; Moore, 1990, pp. 62–72). While maintaining civil relations with the Home Office, he was able to use his personal influence with the Home Secretary, Sir Samuel Hoare, to maintain the ban against political processions in the East End of London until the Second World War, against the advice of the Home Office officials (PRO HO 144/21087/367–70). He wished to extend the ban to the whole of London in 1938, but this request was turned down by the

Cabinet, after objections by Home Office officials, and consultation with the opposition (PRO HO 144/21087/208–10, 215–19, 225–31). Hoare had been Trenchard's closest political supporter in the inter-service battles of the 1920s, and the Home Office and Commissioner's files have several congratulatory notes from the Home Secretary, relating to Game's efficient and hardline management of fascist disturbances. The problems associated with the alleged partiality of the police in favour of the fascists in the 1930s, most certainly did not originate in official policy.

If official attitudes were not pro-fascist, local constabularies encountered difficulties over interpretation of the law and the increasing number of situations leading to conflict. Magistrates, too, treated anti-fascist protestors more harshly than fascists (PRO MEPO 2/3109, MEPO 2/3115). The attitudes of individual policemen meant that an even-handed approach to fascists and anti-fascists was difficult to implement. 'H' Division in Bethnal Green and the constabulary in Shoreditch were particularly notorious for policemen allegedly treating anti-fascist protestors less fairly than fascists.

Although some policemen were cautioned or disciplined for not arresting blatantly abusive anti-Semitic speakers, Game was forced to admit that the tactics of the fascists kept most of them within the law, which was difficult to enforce (PRO MEPO 2/3127). Game complained that attempts to prosecute anti-Semitic speakers foundered on the belief of the Director of Public Prosecutions that proceedings would probably fail because the fascists had developed the technique of criticizing the Jewish people as a whole, rather than those present at the meeting (PRO HO 144/21381/86). While Sir John Simon and Game repeatedly emphasized the need for the police to be seen to arrest perpetrators of anti-Semitic libels (PRO MEPO 2/3043), the vagueness of the law made it difficult to operate in practice, despite the prohibiting of abusive words and behaviour in section 5 of the Public Order Act which extended the offence from London to the rest of the United Kingdom. Local officers had a difficult task in gauging whether intervention to prevent critical, and arguably abusive, comments by fascists about Jews and communists would create a greater threat of disturbance than ignoring the provocation.

The hostile perception of British fascism by the state was

reinforced by reports from Special Branch and MI5. The former were mainly concerned with the overt behaviour of fascists, particularly monitoring demonstrations and anti-Semitism in the East End of London between 1936 and 1939. The decision to collect intelligence on British fascism was taken at a conference at the Home Office on 23 November 1933, attended by Home Office officials, Lord Trenchard, two representatives from MI5 and Superintendent Canning, the head of Special Branch (PRO HO 45/25386/54–59). At this meeting it was decided not to ban political uniforms, but for information to be systematically collected on fascist movements in the United Kingdom. This would mainly be based on monthly reports from chief constables and the political surveillance of Special Branch and MI5 agents. The material would be analysed within MI5, whose reports would be sent to the Home Office. In essence this meant the BUF was now placed in the same category as the CPGB or so-called front organizations, although its threat to both public order and internal security was seen as less dangerous. As a direct result of the increase in political surveillance this entailed, Trenchard expanded Special Branch from 136 to 200 officers in 1934 (Blake, 1978, p. 228). Since 1931 the police had also been asked to provide the Home Office with details of all disturbances however minor in nature. This was to be in force until 1939 in the Metropolitan Police District.

Special Branch reports took an interactionist perspective of the violence between fascists and communists in the 1930s. Although both fascist and communist violence was portrayed as the work of a criminal and hooligan element, particularly in the East End of London, official fascist reactions were presented in a more neutral manner. Fascists, for the most part, obeyed all police requests without question, and kept the authorities informed of their plans for processions and meetings. Communists were less accommodating, and complained vigorously about police harrassment and infringement of civil rights. Trenchard argued that the problem of fascist–communist violence was amongst the most difficult he ever had to deal with. He recognized that although the fascists obeyed the letter of the law, their practice of holding meetings in close proximity to centres of high concentration of Jews and communists meant these two groups were often understandably incensed by the fascist presence. Even he recognized the problem of patrolling the borderline of the excesses of freedom of speech, and the injustice of punishing those provoked rather than the provokers. This needs to be realized when analysing police records, which show the much higher number of arrests of anti-fascists than fascists (cf. Cullen, 1993, pp. 245–67).

Special Branch tended to assume that all left-wing and radical anti-fascist organizations, which were not explicitly aligned to the Labour Party, were communist front organizations, that were directly or indirectly controlled by the Comintern in Moscow. They were even suspicious of populist independent non-political anti-fascist groups, which were not aligned to respectable law-abiding organizations, such as the Democratic Union and the Legion of Democrats. These were not regarded as genuine movements by Special Branch, but groups run by confidence tricksters, who were mainly concerned with pocketing financial contributions from the public (PRO MEPO 2/3043).

The MI5 reports, too, are very informative with regard to official attitudes to public order. They particularly stress the constitutional implications for Mosley's adherents of supporting the BUF. For MI5, public order disturbances, such as those following the Olympia meeting of 7 June 1934 and the 'Battle of Cable Street' on 4 October 1936, led to publicity and the growth of extremism in general. Many of the middle and working classes who were worried about unemployment were also attracted to fascism by the argument that Mosley was upholding the right of free speech, and was making a stand against 'red violence' and the disruptive tactics of communists and other radicals at political meetings since the war. Similarly communists could portray their mass demonstrations against the BUF as defending democracy from the threat to constitutional liberties posed by the native form of fascism.

MI5 argued that many of those recruited to fascism were unaware of the central contradiction of the BUF. A party which ostensibly stood for the principle of free speech would, according to its platform, capture power at a general election, which would then be followed by the suppression of all opinion opposed to the fascists (PRO HO 144/20141/306; HO 144/20142/114–15, 216). Like the communists the fascists were patently insincere in using civil rights and democratic arguments to harness support. For the fascists, MI5 argued, force not the rule of law was the basis of political control. F.A. Newsam at the Home Office argued from these reports that if economic conditions deteriorated, and people became more concerned about the threat of unemployment, the BUF could contain the 'seeds of mischief'. Fascism strengthened communism, as it encouraged the growth of a united anti-fascist front (under communist influence), which included individuals who in no other circumstances would appear on the same platform as communists. Newsam also disliked the fact that the necessity of protecting fascists from their enemies was being misrepresented by the communists and other fellow travellers, who argued that the authorities were pro-fascist, and that the law was not being administered impartially (PRO HO 144/20142/211–12). Newsam was adamant that there was absolutely no truth in these allegations.

MI5 argued that the contradictions within the BUF led to a high turnover of membership, and after an initial surge, the Olympia meeting had proved a decisive setback for Mosley. This was not due to the communist opposition to the meeting, but to Conservative MPs, the national press and other expressions of public opinion, which made Mosley abandon his policy of using his Blackshirts to overwhelm interrupters (PRO HO 144/20142/225). While adopting the techniques of low politics, Mosley was not prepared to challenge the large body of public opinion, which resented the determination of the fascists to use unlimited force to eject interrupters from their meetings (PRO HO 144/20142/222). Similarly MI5 saw the failure of Mosley to make more capital from the East End campaign as a result of either his incapacity or unwillingness to challenge the law, or the threat of new legislation (PRO HO 144/20162/404).

The attitude of the authorities then to fascist-inspired problems of public order was not a simple one. The state recognized that political anti-Semitism was as potent a source of conflict as fascist–communist disturbances, and was equally concerned to defuse this related issue. The Public Order Act was to take an even-handed approach to this problem as well.

If the authorities were nervous, hesitant and often divided about further restricting civil liberties, the same was true in their attitude towards immigration and anti-Semitism. The authorities viewed political liberty as a precious flower which was constantly threatened by issues like unemployment and immigration, which could be whipped up by political extremists to influence the masses against the government. The nervousness about extremism also became manifest during the abdication crisis, when despite political consensus across the political spectrum not to form a 'King's party' in support of Edward VIII, MI5 became worried about BUF support for the king (PRO HO 144/20710/38–42).

While the authorities trusted the ability of the democratic electorate to see through the false claims of extremists under normal conditions, they became far less confident if the political system was seen to be in crisis. This led to a schizophrenic attitude. In the 1930s the state's reaction to the fascist anti-Semitic campaign highlighted the contradiction between political asylum for those fleeing persecution on the continent, and increasing restrictionist pressures on immigration caused by establishment fears of working-class unrest as a result of increased competition for employment and housing. One such alarmist view came from Sir Philip Game, who despite Home Office scepticism, expressed the fear that any influx of refugees coming from the continent might bring the political extremes together: the fascists who had been attacking the Jews for three years, and the communists who might argue that Jewish refugees were taking away gentile employment (PRO HO 144/21381/186; Cross, 1977, pp. 284–5).

The state also feared any mass reaction to changes in the law which would specifically protect minorities, even against the most vicious forms of racist propaganda. This was made clear in the government response to the *Rex* v. *Leese* case in 1936. Unlike the summary jurisdiction of magistrates' courts used to regulate public order, Leese was indicted on charges of seditious libel and creating a public mischief in September 1936. Leese was 'Director-General' of the Imperial Fascist League, which was Mosley's most significant, if unsuccessful, fascist rival in the 1930s. In February 1936 Leese's newspaper, *The Fascist*, had alleged that the Jews practised ritual murder against Christian children. Leese was found not guilty of seditious libel by the jury (PRO HO 45/24967/52). Leese still went to prison for six months because he refused to pay a small fine.

The Attorney-General was astonished at the verdict, and

concluded that the jury viewed Leese as a stupid crank with honest convictions who should be found not guilty of the serious charge of seditious libel. The Home Office viewed this as a precedent, and resisted all attempts to include specific clauses with respect to racial incitement in the Public Order Act. Unless it could be proved to have provoked disorder the authorities refused to prosecute even the worst cases of anti-Semitic or racist libel.

What was also interesting in the state's response to violence and anti-Semitism was the administrative concern of Whitehall to avoid the impression of reacting to pressure from street politics. Whilst proper attention at all times was made to secure the support of the opposition, particularly the Labour Party, to proposed changes in legislation, care was also taken to encourage a proper distance between Labour and more left-wing opinions, and to avoid any connections between the Home Office and what were deemed CPGB front organizations.

With regard to political anti-Semitism the support of the moderate Board of Deputies of British Jews (BDBJ), as the leaders of Jewish public opinion, was cultivated, and government distanced itself from the militant Jewish People's Congress (JPC). Similarly no deputation from the NCCL to protest about aspects of the Public Order Act was allowed, on the grounds that such opinions expressed had been fully discussed in Parliament during the report stage of the Bill.

An additional reason was given in a Home Office minute, however. This argued that both the JPC and NCCL were alleged to have 'close subterranean connections' with the CPGB, particularly through the NCCL's secretary, Ronald Kidd. Although distinguished persons were vice presidents of the NCCL, and it ostensibly had laudable aims, it vilified the police and alleged they displayed partiality to fascists in the East End of London. The BDBJ had also made it clear that the JPC was not a body which commanded respect in responsible Jewish quarters. The Home Office pointed out that at the JPC delegate conference one of the speakers argued that fascist violence should be met with counter-violence in the streets. Both organizations appeared to oppose fascism as a political philosophy, and for the government to receive a deputation from organizations who wished to prevent the lawful propagation of a political creed might be open to misrepresentation (PRO MEPO 2/3112; MEPO 3/553).

The hostility towards the NCCL was also shown with regard to its report on the Thurloe Square demonstration in March 1936, when a police charge broke up an anti-fascist rally. The problems associated with this led the government to be very careful about limiting the right of marches and processions in the Public Order Act. In spite of 46 complaints listed by the NCCL, Sir Philip Game argued that he had a 'great deal of evidence' on the other side, and then partially contradicted himself by admitting he had only five witnesses, two of whom were police inspectors. Nevertheless with two MPs and Lord Dawson of Penn, the police case had 'quality' on its side. He then accused Kidd of manufacturing the case against the police through coaching witnesses at the NCCL enquiry (PRO HO 45/25463/36–53).

Such attitudes preserved the story that Whitehall did not respond to low politics pressure groups, particularly those which could be portrayed as subject to extremist influence. The reality of the situation was somewhat more complex. The NCCL was fully aware that its direct influence on official circles was counter-productive. However, its indirect pressure was much more important. Both Labour and the Liberals were receptive to some of the arguments about the threat to freedom put forward by the NCCL, so opposition MPs were cultivated. While political influence originated in a variety of sources there can be little doubt that the NCCL played an important role in articulating some of the constitutional concerns which affected the opposition's view of the government's legislation with regard to public order and internal security in the 1930s. As the government tried to formulate new legislation in these areas with as much political consensus as possible the views of the opposition were important on such matters and led to significant changes in proposed legislation. This was a particular concern for the government after public hostility had been voiced about the Incitement to Disaffection Act in 1934, when the Admiralty and MI5 persuaded the state to stamp down on communist anti-militarist propaganda. Whilst opposition to some aspects of legislation could not be placated, and the NCCL went over the top in its concern for the defence of cherished liberties, it nevertheless remained true that it had more influence than its cursory and hostile treatment by the authorities would suggest. Whilst Whitehall was keen to preserve the image that low politics did not influence decision-making, fascist–communist violence in the 1930s, and its political management by the state, was influenced indirectly by what happened on the streets.

The denigration of extra parliamentary pressure does not change the fact that the authorities were equally concerned with preserving civil liberties as their critics, and that they acted with hesitation and reluctance to alter the law. The fact that Sir Thomas Inskip, the Attorney-General, advised against banning hunger marches in 1932, that the opposition were not fully supportive of the public order legislation and that the position suddenly improved after July 1934 were the chief reasons why the law was not altered after the major public order disturbances of the early 1930s. It took the problem posed by the Battle of Cable Street on 4 October 1936, the state preparations for the 1936 hunger march and possible threats to public order posed by the abdication crisis in December 1936 to force the government to change the law and bring forward aspects of previously proposed legislation, which was hastily cobbled together in a Cabinet inter-departmental committee to form the Public Order Act of 1936.

This legislation was in fact addressing wider concerns than that provoked by fascist/communist violence and political anti-Semitism in the 1930s, but the Battle of Cable Street acted as the catalyst for bringing forward such legislation. Certainly its first two clauses banning political uniforms and paramilitary formations had the BUF very much in mind. But the increase of controls by the authorities, of the regulation of public processions and demonstrations in Clause 3 and the tightening of legislation with regard to the carrying of offensive weapons at meetings were a response to more general concerns which had arisen since the late nineteenth century. Sections 5 and 6 making abusive words and behaviour an offence throughout the country and giving the chairmen of meetings more powers to enable them to ask the authorities for assistance, if necessary, at public meetings, was related to the behaviour of communists rather than the fascists. It was to be section 5 which was to be used most by the authorities and they were to prosecute far more anti-fascists than fascists.

The Public Order Act proved adequate in containing the problem posed by British fascist provocation in the later 1930s. The police had little trouble in containing fascist–communist confrontations outside the metropolitan police district, and what problems arose mainly concerned the management of processions and demonstrations. Section 3 was used to prevent potential violence in the East End of London, and processions were banned between 1937 and 1949, the requisite ban being renewed every six weeks. This, however, was indirect control by the Home Office, as the Metropolitan Police Commissioner was responsible for requesting its use.

For the state it was the deteriorating international situation, with escalating areas of tension provoked both by fascist Italy and more particularly Nazi Germany that increasingly concerned the authorities. We now know that Mussolini was Mosley's political 'sugar-daddy' between 1933 and 1937, although MI5 and Special Branch sources found little evidence to suggests there was significant outside funding after 1936. A secret BUF bank account was uncovered by Special Branch during the war. This showed that £224,000 had been laundered into BUF funds between 1934 and 1937 as a result of foreign currency transactions (PRO HO 283/10/9). Mosley's explanation that this represented a secure and secret route for British entrepreneurs to give funds to the BUF ignored the fact that a much simpler and cheaper way of financing Mosley, whilst preserving anonymity, would be to send a donation via the account of a third party, Mosley's solicitor.

It was therefore increased concerns about internal security and the threat of the creation of a fifth column or of aiding and abetting Nazi espionage that increasingly worried the security service, and the government, after 1937. As war approached the BUF was reassessed as a security risk rather than as a potential ally in anti-communist operations by MI5. The strange case of Major Vernon, whom John Preen, a BUF member, claimed had burgled a house for the benefit of MI5 to repossess sensitive classified material allegedly being passed on to the Soviets, smacked of both the informal use of right-wing organizations by the security authorities since the First World War and the subcontracting out of dubious and deniable operations.

The intelligence gathered on British fascism represented a fairly competent exercise in political surveillance and it is obvious that the authorities had excellent sources of information. It appears that there were several professional agents operating in the BUF, as well as the usual 'narks' who supplied intelligence titbits for Special Branch. MI5 regarded the BUF as a hybrid organization: it contained a 'revolutionary' wing to which Mosley inclined, and a more acceptable group from MI5's standpoint of right-wing patriots. The most important input was the information from Maxwell Knight and his agents in B5b, which was analysed by F.B. Aiken-Sneath in 1939–40. Knight himself had been Director of Intelligence in the BF and in 1935 another MI5 agent, a 'P.G. Taylor', became head of the Industrial Department and the 'Z' (Intelligence) organization of the BUF (PRO HO 144/20144/137). According to information in the Aubrey Lees personal file his real name was James McGuirk Hughes (PRO HO 283/45). Francis Hawkins argued that Maxwell Knight used his brother-in-law to spy on him in the office (PRO HO 283/40/22).

There have also been claims that there were agents in fundraising and the secretarial staff. One or more of these agents was presumably the source of a large number of leaks, details of financial expenditure and reports of BUF administration meetings in the 1930s (PRO HO 144/20144/135–39). Thus MI5 were in a perfect position to analyse British fascism in the 1930s, as they ran the BUF's intelligence network, had agents perfectly placed to spy on the administration, and Knight himself had controlled the intelligence section of the most important precursor of Mosley's organization. Whatever the role played by MI5 in the formation of Britain's first fascist movement, the merger of the BF with the BUF in 1932 represented a launching pad for the successful infiltration of Mosley's organization.

Nicholas Mosley has stated that his father was fully aware that one of his main backers, W.E.D. Allen, was an MI5 agent (Mosley, 1983, pp. 174–5). John Hope has suggested he was in fact the principal MI6 agent in the BUF, a case supported by his role as head of station in Ankara during the war. As he already knew about Taylor's activities, it appears that Mosley recognized the extent to which the BUF had been infiltrated (Thurlow, 1994, p. 206). Sir Oswald Mosley later argued that Allen was a Walter Mitty figure whose information would have been unreliable. In fact Allen appears to have been intimately involved with the most secretive of BUF's activities in the 1930s, being one of the three signatories in whose name the secret bank account was opened. He was also involved with Mosley's attempt to corner the market in commercial radio franchises in the 1930s, including a highly controversial deal with Hitler in 1938, in an attempt to provide funds for the BUF (PRO HO 283/13/107–10). Mosley always maintained there was nothing illegal in BUF activities, and the fact that intelligence agents were deliberately involved in several of the more questionable activities suggests that Mosley played a complex intelligence game with the authorities.

The role then of the state in the failure of the British Union of Fascists was a fairly complex one. While other factors like how Mosley misconceived the nature of the crisis in British society in the inter-war period, why the BUF was perceived as an undesirable foreign import and alien to the liberal, pluralistic political culture, and the personnel, organizational and ideological weaknesses of the movement accounted for its inability to emerge from the political fringe, the state used both direct and indirect methods to isolate the party (Thurlow, 1989, pp. 67–84; Susser, 1988). The state authorities – the uniformed police and the security service – were used to put the BUF under political surveillance. Informal pressure was also applied to ensure that British fascism received as little publicity as possible in a free society, and following incidents where that was no longer feasible, 'blaming the Blackshirts' would be the message that would be conveyed in the media (Thurlow, 1993, pp. 112–29). When such relatively sophisticated social control was in danger of breaking down after the 'Battle of Cable Street', stengthening the legal weapons at the disposal of the authorities was the preferred option.

It should be noted, however, that the state moved very cautiously and with the maximum degree of consensus before the law was tightened. While the authorities were particularly concerned to ensure that most public order disturbances were kept within the jurisdiction of magistrates' courts, they were confident enough to expect that minimal penalties for transgression of regulations would ensure continued social control in the 1930s. The assumptions behind this included the reluctance to allow juries to consider public order transgressions, and the justified belief in the respect of the law by the majority of citizens. The point was that despite the surface froth of communist–fascist and political anti-Semitism disturbances, particularly in the East End of London during the later 1930s, the authorities controlled proceedings with a minimal degree of violence ensuing, despite the reporting of over 1000 political meetings in each of the summer months in the Metropolitan Police district between 1936 and 1939. Whilst police resources were stretched to the limit, and large numbers of special constables were drafted in for routine duties, numbers prosecuted were relatively low, although far more anti-fascists than fascists were convicted of public order offences.

The evidence suggests that political violence in the 1930s was relatively easily contained by the authorities, and that there were no proven fatalities resulting from such disturbances, and no British Horst Wessel. It took the renewed public order concerns, combined with problems relating to internal security during the Second World War which culminated in the fifth column scare of spring 1940, to force the authorities to intern 747 members of the BUF, and to outlaw the organization on 10 July 1940. From these two blows the BUF was never to recover. Compared with France, and the illiberal measures suffered by Japanese-Americans during the war, the treatment by the British state of fascists – and communists – in 1939 was remarkably tolerant. It was ironic that the authorities moved first against German aliens, the vast majority of whom were anti-Hitler refugees or Jews, rather than against the alleged British fifth column. Even then, although the state was directly responsible for the closing down of British fascism during the Second World War, it took the crisis of May 1940 for the state to intervene, and the reluctance of the Home Office to fall in line with the security authorities to sanction detention without trial was to lead to continuing tension with MI5 and the Security Executive throughout the war (Simpson, 1992, pp. 115–200; Thurlow, 1994, pp. 243–57).

The point, however, is that British fascism had failed long before 1940. From its inception in October 1932 to its peak of between 40,000 and 50,000 members in July 1934, it remained of only marginal significance to British politics. Its main function during the later 1930s was as a political nuisance, whose existence caused public order concerns for the authorities. There is continuing dispute over the size of its recovery, but if armchair supporters are included, then it may have recovered to half its 1934 peak by 1939, although the official Home Office figure in 1940 was about 9000 (Thurlow, 1994, p. 228).

What is not in dispute is the effect of internment on the BUF. The smearing of British fascists as alleged potential traitors, which public opinion read into the fact of fascist internment, meant the impossibility of ever resurrecting the organization, and the blackballing by state and society of any future attempted political comeback by Sir Oswald Mosley. The often barbaric treatment of minorities, the attempted genocide of the Jews in the Holocaust and the horrors of the attempt to create the New Order meant that any organization which could be labelled as fascist or Nazi in Britain would be ostracized and deemed as beyond the pale by public opinion after 1945. British fascism was an abysmal failure before the Second World War. The resolve to destroy absolutely the vestiges of the lunacies of Nazism, through the policy of unconditional surrender, meant that any attempted resurrection of British fascism after 1945 was bound to fail.

REFERENCES

Anderson, G., *Fascists, Communists and the National Government* (Columbia, 1983).
Blake, D., 'Civil disorder in Britain 1910–39. The roles of the government and the military authorities', PhD thesis, University of Sussex, 1978.
Christian, J., *Mosley's Blackshirts* (London, 1986).
Cross, J.A., *Sir Samuel Hoare* (London, 1977).
Cullen, S., 'Political violence: the case of the British Union of Fascists', *Journal of Contemporary History*, Vol. 28, No. 2, 1993, pp. 245–67.
Drennan, J., *BUF, Oswald Mosley and British Fascism* (London, 1934).
Foott, B., *Dismissal of a Premier: The Philip Game Papers* (Sydney, 1968).
Hansard, HC Deb 5s.
Hinsley, F.H. and Simkins, C.A.G., *British Intelligence in the Second World War. Volume IV. Security and Counter-Intelligence* (London, 1990).
Hope, J.G., 'British Fascism and the British state 1917–27: a reassessment of the documentary evidence', *Labour History Review*, Vol. 57, No. 3, 1992, pp. 72–83.
Hope, J.G., 'Fascism and the state in Britain: the case of the British Fascists', *Australian Journal of Politics and History*, Vol. 39, No. 3, 1993, pp. 367–80.

Hope, J.G., 'Surveillance or Collusion? Maxwell Knight, MI5 and the British Fascisti', *Intelligence and National Security*, Vol. 9, No. 4, 1994, pp. 651–75.

Jones, T. and K. Middlemas, *Whitehall Diary Vol. 2* (Oxford, 1969).

Lewis, D., *Illusions of Grandeur* (Manchester, 1987).

Moore, A., 'Sir Philip Game's "other life": the making of the 1936 Public Order Act in Britain', *The Australian Journal of Politics and History*, Vol. 36, No. 1, 1990, pp. 62–72.

Morgan, J., *Conflict and Order* (Oxford, 1987).

Mosley, N., *Beyond the Pale* (London, 1983).

Public Record Office (Kew): HO, FO, MEPO series.

Simpson, A.W.B., *In the Highest Degree Odious* (Oxford, 1992).

Susser, L., 'Fascist and anti-fascist attitudes in Britain between the wars', DPhil thesis, University of Oxford, 1988.

Thurlow, R., 'The failure of British fascism 1932–40', in Thorpe, A. (ed.), *The Failure of Political Extremism in Interwar Britain* (Exeter, 1989), pp. 67–84.

Thurlow, R., *Fascism in Britain* (Oxford, 1987).

Thurlow, R., 'Blaming the Blackshirts: the authorities and the anti-Jewish disturbances in the 1930s', in Panayi, P. (ed.), *Racial Violence in Britain 1840–1950* (Leicester, 1993), pp. 112–29.

Thurlow, R., *The Secret State* (Oxford, 1994).

Trenchard Papers, RAF Museum, Colindale.

West, W.J., *Truth Betrayed* (London, 1987).

4 Oswald Mosley and the Union Movement: Success or Failure?
Anne Poole

> The puzzle about fascism since the War is that it has survived at all. Even in the defeated fascist states, the climate after 1945 was overwhelmingly hostile to the extreme right. Fascism carried the stink of humiliating defeat and destruction, and the memory of colossal crimes committed by the Nazis was still fresh in the minds of millions who had suffered at their hands.
>
> (Wilkinson, 1981, p. 10)

In 1945 European fascists and Nazis were faced with the pressing question of how to ensure the survival of an ideology that was stigmatized by past associations and, in the case of Nazi Germany, a history of unrivalled criminality and inhumanity. The inquiry we must make is why did the Union Movement (UM) fail to achieve success in Great Britain as a mass political party in the period 1948-66?

Before we seek to answer such a question we might do well to ponder what is meant by success? UM did indeed fail electorally and certainly never attracted a mass membership. However, it would be wrong to conclude that this was Oswald Mosley's only aim with UM. He has been written off as a power-seeking cynic committed to attaining a central political position at any cost, and this is true to a certain extent. There was, though, far more to his ideas and actions than this simplistic interpretation of his motivation. He and many others believed, and still believe, that they have found the ideal political system which would ensure the personal fulfilment and peaceful and happy lives of the worthy few, if not for the many deemed unworthy and unwanted. That the ideas and ideals of fascism are still current and seemingly viable in certain quarters is witness to the fact that Mosley succeeded in his primary aim to regenerate and perpetuate the fascist creed. His success lies in the legacy of ideas and the methods used for their dissemination rather than as the leader of a mass movement. This chapter will look at the electoral failure of Mosley and UM and also consider the ways and at what level they might be considered to be a success. The conclusions that are drawn at this stage must be seen as tentative and as pointing the way for further research, as little scholarship yet exists in this area.

FAILURE

Husbands (1992) has suggested that there are four major types of explanation proposed for the failure of the extreme right in Great Britain. These explanations can be categorized as economic, cultural, political, and leadership and organizational theories. Those who propose economic arguments focus on the belief that conditions have never been sufficiently dire in Britain, even in the Great Depression of the 1930s, to allow the growth of widespread support. Adherents to the culture-based causal interpretations of failure consider that the 'British people' are more tolerant of 'outsiders' and display a marked commitment to the 'rules of the democratic game'. The role of the first-past-the-post electoral system plays the major part for the exponents of political theories. Finally, the leadership qualities, organizational deficiencies and the tendency to schism feature most often in the last category. However, it is impossible to attribute the blame for the failure of UM as a mass party to any one of these individual theories alone. It is more appropriate to suggest a multicausal explanation in which all these factors can be said to have played a part in differing degrees.

PRE-UNION ACTIVITIES

The British Union of Fascists and National Socialists (BUF) was closed down by the government in July 1940 and it was never to emerge under this title again. Prior to this on 23 May Sir Oswald Mosley and 25 prominent fascists were interned under Defence Regulation 18b(1a). By the end of June that year there were 747 British fascists interned (Thurlow, 1994, p. 245).

These men and women were imprisoned without charge or trial because the government considered that they might be capable of 'prejudicial acts against the state' or that they had 'hostile associations'. Although Mosley had published a statement in *Action*, a BUF publication, in September 1939 that 'nothing to injure our country or help any other power' should be done by members of the BUF, it was felt that there was a potential for fifth column activities or worse.

The internment of British fascists was a dark day for liberty in a country that professed to be fighting a war in defence of such an ideal. These people were forced to leave their jobs, homes and families with very little time or opportunity to make provision. There was no recognition from the authorities that many of the families of those interned would be facing financial hardship and the situation was not helped by the verbal abuse and social isolation perpetrated by some of their neighbours and families (Charnely, 1990, p. 157). Most of those detained were released well before the end of the war due to the suspension of habeas corpus. However, sometimes their health was broken; some returned to find broken marriages and many, understandably in the circumstances, faced difficulties in returning to old jobs or finding new employment.

The effect of internment on the political commitment of those who had been members of the BUF appears to have been varied and not necessarily what the government had intended. Some found that their experience merely strengthened their commitment to support Mosley and the cause, but for many their political will was broken and they just wanted a quiet life after their release. As an agency of reinforcement it certainly furnished some with a '*freikorps* spirit' and a greater determination to dedicate themselves to the cause of a 'new Europe arising phoenix-like from the ashes of the old' (Hamm, 1983, p. 111). But for others the experience provided the opportunity for 'for intensive political discussions . . . an analysis of the past' which focused on the authoritarian aspects of Mosley's leadership and the more negative consequences of this (BUF member quoted in Linehan, 1992, p. 457). As a result a number of the internees deserted Mosley and the movement, some returned to obscurity, and others to more nationalist groups such as the League of Empire Loyalists. Thurlow (1987, p. 189) goes so far as to claim that 'internment destroyed British fascism and its later resurrection in various revisionist or derivative forms was compromised from the outset by the smear of necessity for preventive detention for fascists in the Second World War.' Mosley and UM were to continue to suffer from this 'leakage' of membership throughout the life of the movement.

Certainly membership was never as high as during the 1930s. It is notoriously difficult to put an exact number on this as Mosley saw no reason to give the 'enemy' information if it was not necessary. Some have, however, attempted an estimation and the general consensus is that during the period under discussion active membership can be estimated at between 1000 and 1500, with inactive supporters numbering anything up to 15,000 (Lewis, 1987; Thurlow, 1987; Lunn and Thurlow, 1980; Skidelsky, 1975; Walker, 1977; Foot, 1965; Cross, 1961). The majority of these were undoubtedly former BUF members, apart from a burst of enthusiasm from a few 'teddy boys' in the late 1950s. As the 1930s party was characterized by the youth of its leadership, so UM's was to be by the age of its membership.

The 18b Detainees (British) Aid Fund was a registered war charity which was established by some of the members of the BUF who had not been interned to raise funds to provide assistance to the families of those who were 'less fortunate' than themselves. The charity claimed to be a non-political organization and it arranged dances, socials, concerts and non-political meetings to generate money. It has, however, been proposed that the 18b (British) Detainees Fund was a 'front' to hide the activities of its organizers (PRO H045/25124; Mullally, 1946; Hope, 1993). It is suggested that the charity became a rallying centre for former BUF members, ex-18b detainees and other fellow travellers, and that it provided a coordinating force to ensure the continued existence of fascist ideas and, ultimately, a rebirth of the movement after the war. This is confirmed by the comment to the Cabinet by Home Secretary Herbert Morrsion, that he considered that the purpose of the organization was to 'serve as the nucleus for the political party until the ban on the BUF is raised' (PRO CAB 66/35 WP(43)148, 14 April 1943). This position is also corroborated by a report on 'Fascist matters' contained in the Vansittart papers (Vnst II 1/24). The evidence seems to leave little doubt about the twin purposes of the organization.

Sir Oswald Mosley was released from gaol on 20 November 1943 on the grounds of ill-health, having been interned for over three years. He used his period of imprisonment to learn German and to read widely including the Greek and German classics. Mosley was to claim his time in prison was a period of reflection which was to be followed and complemented by political activism. This is in accord with his idea of the need for 'Thought Deed Men' – an elite body of individuals who could not only reflect and reason but also act. Three doctors had concluded that his health would suffer permanently or that he might even die if he continued to suffer the deprivations of prison life. Ironically, as Martin Walker points out (Walker, 1987, p. 23), Mosley was to survive longer than any member of the Cabinet that interned him. It seems that there was an element of political calculation in the decision to release him. It was felt that Mosley had been branded a traitor by his internment and as such was discredited in the eyes of the British public; were he to die in prison, he could become a martyr to the cause of fascism which could then become a permanent feature of the British political landscape (HC Deb, vol. 395, col. 1660, quoted in Skidelsky, 1975, p. 461).

There was an immediate public outcry stimulated in no small degree by the Communist Party of Great Britain (CPGB). An accompanying press campaign to 'Put Mosley Back in Gaol' ensured the extension and maintenance of public concerns. Mosley and other released BUF members continued to be subject to government restrictions until the end of the war. These limitations did not prevent Jeffrey Hamm, BUF member in the 1930s and Mosley's political secretary after the death of Raven Thompson in 1955, from joining the British League of Ex-Servicemen, an organization founded in 1937 by a James Taylor. Hamm had come upon a one-time BUF member at Speaker's Corner in Hyde Park who had been interned with Taylor. Hamm could see no reason why 'we should not join this organisation and campaign for ex-service rights, while extending its platform to include a defence of Mosley, and to prepare for his return to active politics' (Hamm, 1983, p. 136).

This organization was to be the core of most political activism on the streets for former BUF members directly after the war. Its title was extended to include women, and activities included street corner meetings – sometimes three or four a week; a monthly publication entitled *The British League Review*; the sale of Mosley's current publications; and Hamm's own contributions. These comprised pamphlets entitled *Challenge the Old Gang* (Hamm, undated) and *Britain Awake* (Hamm, undated) which contained the usual inter-war Mosleyite themes about the decadence of the 'Old Gang' and some barely hidden anti-Semitism (PRO HO 45/24467). Covert messages were conveyed from Mosley about keeping up the good work (Metropolitan Police Report, No. 123, PRO HO 45/24470). At the time there was much government and public concern about such a prompt return to the streets of London of fascist activity. Mosley, who was acutely aware that the public face of any new movement would have to be scrupulously clean and unblemished by any hint of past difficulties, had given warnings to the League about the anti-Semitic nature of some of the speeches made by Hamm at public meetings (Metropolitan Police Special Branch Report, PRO HO 45/24468).

The CPGB were not the only group to monitor a potential revival in fascist operations. The Independent Labour Party (ILP), National Council for Civil Liberties (NCCL), Trades Union Congress (TUC) and the Jewish community all maintained a watchful eye. The Jewish interest in Mosley and others with a dubious past who were active on the streets was naturally intensified by the revelations about Nazi atrocities in the war. There was a high level of Jewish anti-fascist activity evidenced by the extremely detailed and seemingly accurate surveys produced at the time of fascist and anti-Semitic activities. These were published and circulated to the press and state agencies (Jewish Information Office, 1946; Rose, 1947 and 1948). All these groups involved in the anti-fascist campaigns made it their business to ensure the government was kept up to date with information presumed relevant and they lobbied for action to stem any revival. As early as autumn 1945 the Association of Jewish Ex-Servicemen (AJEX) was active on the streets of London addressing the crowds at Hyde Park's Speaker's Corner. The newspapers of the period contain headlines such as 'Fascists Crawl Out Again Here' (*Daily Mirror*, 28 June 1945), whipping up public concerns and condemning government inaction.

However, Cabinet discussions concluded, after much deliberation, that to ban any renewal of fascist activities would not be in keeping with the spirit of democracy. Furthermore, this would involve coming to terms with a precise definition of fascism – a perennial problem. It was therefore decided to keep a close eye on the developing situation using government surveillance techniques. This stance was not only to raise questions in Parliament and in the minds of the British public but was also to provoke queries at the international level. In Moscow concerns were sounded about the revival of British fascism being conducted with the full knowledge of, and possibly even condoned by, the British government (*Bolshevik*, No. 8, 1947). Among the newly released files at the Public Record Office are several containing tens of petitions with hundreds of signatures to the Home Secretary of the day, Chuter Ede, demanding a ban on any resurgence of the phenomenon (PRO HO 45/24470). It has to be said, though, that a good many of these were from trade unions and left-wing organizations and were perhaps not too indicative of public opinion in general.

Spring 1946 saw the birth of another Jewish anti-fascist organization: the '43 Group – its name inspired by the number of its original members. Maurice Beckman, a founder member of the group, stresses its combative nature (Beckman, 1993) and as in the 1930s meetings became known for their violence rather than the speeches made. The group's tactics included heckling, but only if it was a prerequisite of more destructive action like closing down the speaker's platform. They developed 'commando-style' units to form tightly knit wedges of men to force their way through fascist security at meetings. The group also used 'Aryan-looking' Jews to infiltrate fascist organizations. They appear to have had a considerable amount of success in using the information gleaned to ensure that meetings were cancelled by informing the owners of halls that bookings had been made for fascist meetings using a pseudonym. They even raided fascist book shops in the early hours of the morning to remove and destroy both British and European fascist and Nazi materials.

Jewish attempts to restrict the progress of fascism had also occurred in the 1930s and was to resume again in 1962 with the reformation of the '43 Group, now renamed the '62 Group, and the militant Yellow Star Movement. A riot following a British Movement meeting, timed to coincide with the new legislation on immigration, marked the re-emergence of organized anti-fascist activities. This was followed some three weeks later by a UM rally in Trafalgar Square attended by 7000 people 'most of them there to stop Mosley' (Walker, 1977, p. 42). The rally was abandoned after 15 minutes and there were 15 arrests. There followed a nationwide campaign by anti-fascists to stop Mosley and UM holding meetings and a summer of disruption and violence ensued. Hence anti-fascist activities were a major reason why the movement never managed to make even a moderate advance in establishing themselves as a mass political party. Anti-fascists kept the topic of UM on the agenda if it ever threatened to establish even a tentative hold on the minds of more than a few extremists.

Shortly after his release from gaol Mosley had started a publishing company: Mosley Publications. He denied any interest in taking an active part in politics. This was a business concern which he maintained for many years, later setting up Euphorian Books in Ireland. Mosley published his own and other works in translation. In fact all Mosley's books were published in Germany, selling in greater numbers than they had in Britain. It was an interest he shared with many others in both Britain and on the Continent of a similar political persuasion and level of commitment as himself. The fascist tradition of the importance of the 'idea' was paramount in Mosley's actions in the postwar period. The need for regeneration and propagation was the underlying motive for many of his undertakings.

In his critique of Hitler (Mosley, 1968, pp. 364–73) Mosley considered that Hitler's only crime was hubris – the Greek notion of a mortal presuming God-like status and powers. His concern was that fascism, the 'idea', had been tarnished by its acquaintance with a man whose will was ineffective. It was imperative to work towards the rehabilitation of its image and to disguise the old themes under a thin veneer of respectability. He was also conscious that the BUF in the 1930s had concentrated on the activist element in the party and, unlike Continental fascism, had neglected to court the intelligentsia. This was considered a weakness and in recognition that any new movement would have to fill this vacuum and appeal to the intellectual element, the emphasis was on book and university clubs, discussion groups, a Mosley news letter, and renewed links with Continental fascists and Nazis as a means of disseminating new and old ideas. It is important to recognize that the

UM was not just a movement of political activists at the street level; it was also an intellectual coterie of like minded individuals who came together to ensure the 'idea' did not die.

UNION MOVEMENT

Despite all the debate at the time and the fact that Mosley had denied any involvement with pre-UM activities he has himself clarified the situation in his autobiography. He confirms that: 'Directly the war was over and I was free to move anywhere in Britain I began the organisation of a political movement' (Mosley, 1968, p. 432). The publicity and propaganda surrounding the launch of UM on 7 February 1948 states that the occasion denoted the coming together of 51 organizations. These included members of the 18b Detainees (British) Aid Fund, the League of Ex-Servicemen and women, the Mosley Book Clubs and Discussion Groups and numerous other provincial organizations (Thurlow, 1987, p. 243) who all professed allegiance to Mosley and the cause.

Mosley was acutely aware of the need to distance, at least publicly, himself and his movement from its own murky past and the tainted image of National Socialism and European fascism. There are two dominant themes in the popular and collective memory of the Second World War in Britain which remain constant. One is the positive memory of the Battle of Britain, Dunkirk and the 'blitz spirit' – the people of Britain pulling together as one nation in a fight against the dark and satanic evils of Nazism and fascism. The second is the alien and malevolent, inhuman and nightmare world of Belsen and the Polish death camps associated with Hitler and his Nazi henchmen. Mosley and UM belonged to the second and darker strand. They were outsiders and pariahs.

Consequently, attempts were made to alter the movement's image but with limited success. The old BUF symbol of a bolt of lightning contained in a circle, the 'flash-in-the-pan', was retained, although now it was to signify Mosley's new idea of 'European action with European union' rather than 'British action within British union' (Hamm, 1983, p. 160). The movement's official publication was renamed *Union* but incorporated the title of *Action* which had been the name of the old

BUF paper (it was later to resume its original name). The fascist salute was officially abandoned on account of its close association with Hitler and Mussolini whose posturings all had witnessed on wartime newsreels. However, there is a photograph in *Union* (No. 294, 19 December 1953) of Mosley and his followers using the fascist salute in an East End pub under the headline 'East London greets Mosley'.

The military image of the pre-war BUF had been severely curtailed by the Public Order act of 1936 which had banned the wearing of uniforms by political organizations. This meant that the black uniform worn by the elite active membership which contributed much to the movement's 'public persona' was lost. However, there is evidence in an internal circular of 1956 to suggest that attempts were made to impose some uniformity on UM members' appearance by insisting on a strict dress code when taking part in marches (*Searchlight* file: UM 2.420.3). Marching itself might be perceived as militaristic particularly when highly regimented and when led by a colour party and drum corps accompanied by colour escorts as was the march to Trafalgar Square in July 1956. There was a strong element of continuity with the past in all this and obviously a failure to sufficiently distance the movement from the visual imagery of the unsavoury history of its predecessors. Hamm (1983, p. 160) acknowledges the 'tactical error' of marching again 'through our old strongholds of East London, with flags flying high and drums beating proudly'.

Mosley did not stand in a general election until 1959. The response of the media, the public, the CPGB, ILP, TUC, NCCL and Jewish anti-fascist groups had all combined to make electoral success highly unlikely. He had been waiting for the advent of an economic and social crisis which would sweep him into power. This is a constant theme in his thought and was often given as a reason to UM members for Mosley's failure to stand in general elections. However, the advent of the 'race riots' in August and September 1958 which took place in Nottingham and Notting Hill prompted a return to activist politics. The arrival of the *Empire Windrush* and the ss *Orbita* in 1948 denoted the beginning of 'new commonwealth' immigration in response to the demands of post-war reconstruction and the expansion of the British economy in the 1950s and 1960s which created a shortage of labour which could not be filled by British,

Irish or other European sources (Layton-Henry, 1992, p. 13). There had been a few incidents of racially motivated disorder as early as 1948 but nothing on the scale of the events of late summer 1958. Angry mobs of between 200 and 700 participated in the riots in Notting Hill and some 140 people were arrested.

This provided the opportunity for Mosley's return to parliamentary activity as a candidate for North Kensington. The Mosley had moved to Ireland and bought a second home in Paris in the early 1950s to become European and lessen the burden of frequent European journeys. UM's proud claim to be the first to warn of the potential dangers of black immigration revealed a degree of rivalry which many will find distasteful but, undoubtedly, they were one of the earliest to raise the issue (Mosley, 1968, p. 445). The emphasis in UM literature from the early 1950s onwards, on black immigrants as criminals, sexually promiscuous and carriers of disease, has echoes of Hitler's rhetoric about the undesirability of alleged Jewish defects and provided a model for later extreme right groups to follow. Mosley conducted a speaking tour in October 1958 capitalizing on the riots. However, this was a complete failure due to the cancellation of most of the meetings by the Labour councils who had control of the civic halls where he had been expected to speak.

The headline in *Action* (No. 41, 4 April 1959) states that in the election Mosley would stand for 'Europe-A-Nation', 'Europe-Africa' and 'European Socialism'. This was broadly the programme which had been outlined in 'The objects of the Union Movement' (see *Union*, 14 February 1948, p. 2) and *The Alternative* (1947a). There was a repetition of many of the old BUF policies but these were supplemented with a commitment to European kinship and nationalism; an African Empire to support the new European nation; a novel economic wage–prices policy; and a pretence to democracy beneath the surface of which lurked 'state compulsion as the final arbiter in all matters' (Lewis, 1987, p. 239). At street level the campaign was fought on an anti-immigrant platform with the concomitant theme of white social deprivation aggravated by the 'black influx', Mosley's key idea, and one of separation or apartheid. He considered that it was impossible for different races to live together and for both to prosper. In 1959 he argued that those 'coloured' immigrants who had arrived in Britain since 1945 should return to their homelands with adequate compensation and with British investment in local industry to encourage prosperity in their native lands. He even said the skills that had been learnt in Britain could be used in the development of local industries and so of a healthy native economy (Davidson, 1959, p. 30).

UM put a massive effort into the campaign with Mosley speaking at four or five meetings a night and putting up to 200 canvassers onto the street at the weekend. An eve of election poll had prompted anticipation of a victory based on gaining between 32.5 and 37 per cent of the vote (*Action*, No. 55, 17 October 1959). The actual result was abject failure with Mosley polling only 2821 out of a total of 35,000 votes, or 8.2 per cent and as a consequence he lost his deposit. The average turnout had been 78 per cent whereas in North Kensington it was only 67 per cent and this was to prompt Mosley to seek a judicial enquiry. At a hearing before Mr Justice Slade and Mr Justice Streathfield it was concluded that there had been a breach of the rules, but that this had not materially affected the result and was thus allowed to stand. UM candidates also fought occasional by-elections with a notable lack of success. Mosley was to stand in one more general election in 1966 as a candidate for Shoreditch and Finsbury where he polled 1600 votes, a meagre 4.6 per cent of the total. Three other UM candidates also fought the election with Mosley and together they attracted on average 3.7 per cent of the vote. This was to mark the end of Mosley's involvement in British parliamentary politics and the UM was to decline thereafter, becoming a small group of old retainers committed to keeping Mosley's ideas alive.

In local elections UM fared little better. Mosley states that local elections were fought on the initiative of local branches with little involvement from the party executive. The first candidates stood in 1949 mainly in London, when the movement fielded 15 who managed to attract only 1993 votes between them and 14 of whom came bottom of the poll (Walker, 1977, p. 26). *Union* pronounced this a resounding success under the headline 'Kensington Achievement'. It declared that two of the candidates had polled 1200 votes between them (*Union*, No. 61, 23 April 1949). This was to form the pattern for the movement's strategy and success rate. Campaigns were fought mainly in

London with the occasional foray by those outside the metropolis, but UM never won a seat. The local and national media ridiculed the candidates, their policies and their results while *Union* presented all in a glowing light. The paper kept members' spirits from flagging by reminding them that the electoral system in Britain was inequitable to small parties. It noted that the outstanding case of modern history proved that their time would come. The National Socialists had an initial gain of only 12 seats in the Reichstag in 1928 on 2 per cent of votes, but were swept to power five years later. The report also drew attention to the success of Movement Sociale Italiano (MSI) in Italy and Austrian independent parties (*Union*, No. 100, 21 January 1950).

To return to Husband's model with its four categories used to explain the failure of the extreme right in Britain – these were economic, cultural, political, and leadership and organizational arguments, and as has been suggested it is not possible to reduce entirely any explanation for the failure of UM as a mass party to one individual cause. The first, economic, relies on the notion that in Britain we have never had an economic depression as severe as that of say, Weimar Germany, with its dire social consequences and destabilizing influence. Certainly the 1950s and 1960s in Britain were a time of prosperity, full employment and rising living standards and there was little prospect of class antagonism with a sated middle and working class. Unlike Germany in 1918 there was no legacy of unemployed ex-servicemen imbued with the frontline spirit that went to make up the disenchanted elements in the Freikorps. We were, in any case, the victors in 1945 and, furthermore, this war was worth fighting for. The birth of the welfare state, instigated by the 1945 Labour government, had introduced the notion of state care from cradle to grave. Despite certain limitations introduced in the early 1950s, it provided the sort of security for those most likely to be attracted by what UM had to offer that was unknown before and looks likely never to be known again. This was a time when Harold Macmillan was able to comment at a Conservative Party rally in 1957 that 'most of our people have never had it so good'. So we can safely conclude that the economic conditions in Britain during the period 1945 to 1966 never even approached the crisis point Mosley was expecting.

The second category is the cultural explanation of which

perhaps Benewick (1971) is the chief proponent. He suggests that the British are committed to the democratic political process which, they perceived, Mosley was not. As has been pointed out the programme of UM was to be implemented within the democratic framework. However, UM could never get away from its relationship with the undemocratic Continental fascism and Nazism and the British people, wisely, it would seem, were not willing to trust Mosley. Fascism was seen as a foreign phenomenon and the wartime propaganda machine had played up the posturing and ranting of Hitler, portraying him as a deranged madman. For many Mosley came from the same mould as a man who had sent millions of innocent men, women and children to their deaths. UM's image and symbolism and Mosley's style of delivering speeches all smacked of the earlier movement and not enough had been done to convince the public otherwise. Mosley and the movement were also tarnished by their enforced association with internment and treachery and what Walker calls the 'where-were-you-in-the-war' tag which it was never to lose. The media focused on this side of things rather than concentrate on Mosley's policies. We might describe this as an early case of 'trial by media' in which Mosley and UM were guilty by association rather than by action. There was an unofficial embargo on Mosley's writing and potential television appearances right up until the publication of his autobiography in 1968 and both Hamm and Mosley were to make complaints to the Press Council and High Court respectively. The British government had been right in its assessment that Mosley and his disciples had been stigmatized beyond redemption: they were simply on the wrong side – the losers.

Anti-fascist activity is perhaps one of the most significant reasons for UM failing to build support. The vigilance and organization of these diverse groups is most impressive. The movement was closely monitored and action taken when deemed necessary to prevent any complacency on the part of the authorities. UM meetings were disrupted and cancelled and life made generally difficult for members. Only the most committed stayed the course. The street violence and aggressive tactics associated with these meetings made them unappealing to many and added to the negative perception of the movement. Again newspapers, for ever in search of a story, highlighted the violence, dubious past and foreign flavour of the movement.

Perhaps the most common of the political theories proposed to explain the failure of the extreme right in Britain are those based on the inequity and unrepresentative nature of our first-past-the-post electoral system. As Mosley and *Union* had consistently pointed out, the likelihood of a third party breaking through in Britain is an extremely small one even allowing for the Labour success in 1924. Also the consensual politics of the period meant that the two major parties provided a status quo which encouraged an atmosphere of moderation that did not support radicalism. Furthermore, there was little to attract the electorate in UM's policies. The notion of 'Europe-A-Nation', 'Eurafrica' and 'European Socialism' was either of no interest or beyond comprehension to the average man or woman. Voters may have been concerned by the immigration figures but social conditions were never so poor that people would commit themselves to a man with Mosley's reputation. In any case the mainstream parties were quick to hijack the issue and by 1962 had initiated legislation.

The issue of policy and ideology was also one for UM membership and a cause of schism. The new focus on Europe, rather than the nationalism of the BUF, was a problem for some former and potential members (see Tyndall, 1988). State action towards the BUF and its policy of internment affected membership figures too. A great many ex-BUF men and women had to think long and hard about rejoining Mosley and many chose not to. Even those who did remain committed never felt quite the same optimism about achieving electoral success and the intensity of feeling that had been present in the BUF was gone (Charnely, 1990, p. 203). The vibrant youthful machismo of the earlier days was missing and Hamm talks about a particularly violent meeting where a BUF member removed his false teeth before wading into the mêlée (Hamm, 1983, p. 164).

The authoritarian leadership style of Mosley was responsible for some of the defections. He is accused by one member, in a letter of resignation, of running a personal autocracy more oppressive than fascist Italy or communist Russia (*Searchlight* file: 2.420.1). Certainly the BUF member quoted in Linehan's thesis (1992, p. 457) would appear to confirm this. This idea does conflict somewhat with the fact that Mosley spent most of his time abroad after 1951 and seems to have directed matters from afar through his lieutenants. His lack of involvement in organizational matters was reflected in local election campaigns where he appears to have had little influence. Mosley's absence, and so his lack of direct involvement, must also be considered of some significance when analysing the reasons for the limited success of the movement.

However, perhaps the overwhelming reason for UM's failure was the effect of the Second World War, a total war, on the national psyche. The British people had spent five years manning the Home Front or away fighting. Many had made enormous material sacrifices and lost loved ones. The population had been subjected to a government propaganda machine to demonize the foreign dictators, a campaign which made claims about the nature of the enemy that were to be confirmed by the revelations of Nazi atrocities after the war.

MOSLEY'S LEGACY

There is little doubt, then, that as a mass political party UM was a complete failure. However, to restrict our investigation to this level would be to neglect a side of Mosley and the movement that is of considerable significance. UM had been a vehicle for Mosley's ideas but its slender record of achievement does not mean that Mosley has not left a legacy. The most important legacy we have received from him is his thought which we will now turn to. In the first issue of *Union*, it was declared that like 1848, 1948 was a 'turning point' in the path of history. The former was the year that the 'Old idea' (democracy) was born and the latter marked the birth of the 'New idea' – the new super-national spirit of the age (*Union*, No. 1, 14 February 1948). In this same issue are also published 'The Ten Objects of Union Movement'. The first object of the manifesto was to secure the Union of European peoples, an aim that was first expounded in Mosley's work *The Alternative* (1947a). This was his second publication after the war, *My Answer* (1946) being the first. *My Answer* was essentially an apologia, an attempt at justification of past ideas, policies and actions. *The Alternative*, however, was different.

In a complete reversal of the focus on the nation in his

pre-war works Mosley rejects the idea of nationalism. The Treaty of Versailles had imposed an 'international brotherhood' and the communist insistence on 'replacing the higher with the lower' meant that fascism had been forced into a narrow conception of nationalism. Mosley explains that 'when you are told that you must kiss Harry the Hottentot on both cheeks as a condition of taking a walk down the street you are apt to confine yourself to the close circle of your own family!' (Mosley, 1947b, p. 3). What was needed was a 'Europe-A-Nation', and not a Europe of nations, to stand in opposition to Americanism and Bolshevism.

Mosley claims that he was coming to this conclusion in his 'World Alternative' (Mosley, 1936a). However, there is one distinct difference between *The Alternative* and the 1936 essay. In the latter he is clearly talking about a 'Four Power Bloc of Fascist Nations' which always remain individual entities with their own interests. This is an important distinction as the proposal in *The Alternative* is quite different from Nazi ideas of a German hegemony in a 'European New Order' which Otto Strasser and others supported (Mosley, 1954). Mosley stresses the need for an 'equipe of equals' and not simply a confederation of separate powers. Europe becomes the sovereign nation. However, it is important to note that this is not a new idea. In 1931 the French fascist intellectual Pierre Drieu La Rochelle had published a work entitled *L'Europe contre les patries* with a strikingly similar theme. In 1947 Mosley was insisting that it was time to 'transcend an exclusive nationalism which divides natural friends and relatives ... [to unite] with those nearest to us in blood, tradition, mind and spirit' (Mosley, 1947b, p. 3). What he is suggesting is the extension of patriotism – the idea of European kinship in a sovereign European nation.

The reference to blood links here is an interesting one. It has been argued that in the ideology of the British extreme right there are two strands of thought: on the one hand the more crude biological and Nazi racial discourse of the likes of Arnold Leese, and on the other the less extreme and more sophisticated cultural or Spenglerian contribution of Mosley. The post-war writings of Mosley (and so the ideology of UM) makes this an artificial distinction. There was always the occasional references to the need for birth control in the eugenic spirit (Mosley, 1936b, question 76), the inequality of the races in the Empire (Mosley, 1932, p. 138) and anti-Semitism justified on the basis that the behaviour of some Jews (for Mosley particularly those involved in international finance and anti-fascist activities) merited it. But these were rare and, it is suggested, sentiments expressed by many in British society (Holmes, 1979) – a combination of paternalistic empire racialism and the 'natural' scapegoating of the 'outsider'. In the early post-war period the public reticence of the 1930s, which Mosley returned to in his later years during a period of rehabilitation after the publication of his autobiography in 1968, is something he clearly departs from.

The evidence for this departure can be found in two early post-war publications: *The Alternative* itself and an essay entitled *Union of Europe: Extension of Patriotism: Idea of Kinship* (Mosley, 1947b), a version of which is reproduced at the beginning of *The Alternative*. His argument in the 1947 book contends that racial differences exist and that a European 'great breed' or 'kind' is the culmination of a different and separate strand of evolutionary development to other races (specifically negroes): 'We are favoured by the inestimable blessing of a European race, which is based on millennia of differential development, and possesses the treasure of a unique culture' (Mosley, 1947a, p. 258). He takes, he says, a new 'biological approach' to history. Though he maintains a Spenglerian belief in the superiority of European culture, for Mosley this has become the evidence of hierarchical racial difference.

He discusses the idea of 'Function and Differentiation' (Mosley, 1947a, pp. 255–9). It is important, he argues, to establish the difference between the notion of democratic 'justice' and Platonic 'Justice'. 'Justice' for those who live in a liberal democracy, like Britain, is merely equality before the law which is no equality at all. But 'Justice' for Plato and Mosley is a situation in which all fulfil the function to which they are most naturally fitted to perform. So:

> If it be true that God created men equal, and that they are equal in his sight, it is at least very evident that he equipped them very differently for the only discernible purpose of performing different functions. The leading physicist of the age is differently equipped by nature to a negro boxing

champion; the former is better in the laboratory, the latter in the boxing ring.

(Mosley, 1947a, p. 255)

Here he is talking about individuals but it is interesting to note his failure to qualify the racial pedigree of the leading physicist. However, he goes on to say that, relying on this empirical evidence: 'To recognise the necessity for differentation in function is merely to recognise the facts of life and the laws of nature ... we must accept that differences exist between diverse men and diverse races, which suggest they must perform different functions in life' (Mosley, 1947a, p. 256).

Furthermore, he uses an analogy of the farmer and stockbreeder to stress the importance of not diluting the European 'blood line' and the need to improve it:

> We seek to intensify rather than dilute a good stock when we find it ... we say, 'here is a good strain, keep it, hold it, build on it, develop it' ... an occasional outcross may be valuable, but it should not go outside very similar strains. To render the subject of animal breeding easily intelligible by taking a human parallel, it would not be desirable to go much further, in selecting an outcross with the English type, than a kind as close as the French, German or Scandinavian; or the further Latin types for special purposes.
>
> (Mosley, 1947a, p. 258)

We have established then, for Mosley, there are differences between the races and that these are biologically determined and this is reflected in the different levels of cultural achievement. He writes, in *The Alternative* itself, that this is of no importance and that 'we can set aside the sterile argument whether one is higher and another lower.' However, we must bear in mind that he contradicts this argument in the essay (1947b) where he makes a clear value judgement between 'higher' and 'lower' races. In a section entitled 'Brother Savage' he says that:

> The argument that every savage was in every way the brother and equal of a European just plainly was not true ... the idea that you could build a world on the premise that all men, or all races were equal was a dangerous absurdity ... In

fact they are obviously not equal in intellect, physique, knowledge, achievement, history, or tradition.

(Mosley, 1947b, pp. 2–3)

So in *The Alternative* we find reference to bloodlinks between Europeans which specifically exclude negroes who have followed a different developmental path (he does not discuss other races in this context). These differences are evidenced by 'superior' cultural achievement and 'Justice' requires that each race should be in a role most suited to its development. All this said, it is worth pointing out that the vital difference between Hitler and Mosley is the absence of a social Darwinist element in his thought. For Mosley the historical meta-narrative is not race but 'will'. More specifically the 'will' of certain elite types who have the capability to force the pace of history and evolution. He does not mention whether the black races also possess these elite types or if not whether they will ever reach the point in their development when they might emerge. There is no notion of a struggle between nations and, unlike Hitler and Mussolini, an abhorrence of war. There is never any question then for Mosley of genocide or the 'will to war'. He is, though, undoubtedly a racist in the biological determinist mould because, for Mosley, race determines an individual's nature. The focus on biological determinism combined with his insistence on the role of 'will' is a point of tension in his post-war thought. That an individual's potential is determined, even limited, by his or her race sits ill with the Nietzschean concept of the 'will to power'. If race determines our nature then what is the function of 'will'? The answer may lie in his notion of separate evolutionary strands and the restricted development of the black 'race'.

Mosley's emphasis on the cultural diversity and the undesirability of miscegenation as the basis for racially determined policies is a precursor of the kind of racism that has been used by the new-right to exclude individuals regarded as inferior or different, specifically black immigrants, most notably among those writing for the *Salisbury Review* (see Barker, 1981; Solomos, 1989). UM's programmes and policies reflected Mosley's ideas. The concentration on immigration and the need for repatriation was a consequence of these ideas and cannot be attributed to merely opportunism. As was his suggestion that Africa be developed along mercantilist lines as an empire to support Europe, an idea which he aligned with the 'native policy' of J.B.M. Hertzog in the 'Mosley-Pirow plan' of 1948 (see *Union*, 25 April 1948, pp. 1–2). Hertzog believed, like Mosley, in the supremacy of white civilization and that blacks should be given the opportunity to develop at their own pace in separate black states from which whites were excluded.

A question has arisen about the precise date Mosley wrote *The Alternative*. John Hope has pointed out that there is a certain amount of evidence in the Home Office files and the Vansittart Papers to support the idea that another book exists with a more nationalistic flavour. If there is another book then this would certainly answer questions about the delay in publishing the work. Why had Mosley waited until 1947 to complete the book with his new ideas when he had spent three years in gaol and two years under house arrest with presumably plenty of time on his hands? The answer to this question may be that the reading that Mosley did in gaol may not be the only, or indeed the primary, influence on his post-war thought. Despite Mosley's prudent denials to the Birkett Committee, which was charged with dealing with individuals' appeals against internment, Mosley had always had links with Continental fascists. This has been the subject of much debate which will not be entered into here. However, we can say that he did have contacts with European fascists and Nazis and an insight into the way they were thinking, specifically ex-members of the SS, long before his passport was returned in the summer of 1949 some four years after the end of the war.

Immediately he was free to travel in the summer of 1949 Mosley had visited France, Spain, Tangier and Portugal to see some 'old friends and make new acquaintances'. He met Serrano Suners who had been Foreign Minister of Spain and close members of Franco's family who took him to visit a fascist shrine – the tomb of Jose Antonio Primo de Rivera who had visited Mosley at BUF headquarters in the 1930s and whose 'assassination seemed to me always one of the saddest of the individual tragedies of Europe' (Mosley, 1968, p. 421). He also met Filippo Anfuso, former Italian ambassador to Berlin and final Foreign Secretary in Mussolini's government and a leading light in the MSI. Moreover, the FBI files confirm that UM had a European contact section and a German adviser called Alfred

Francke Kriesche (Gricksch) (CG100–25647, FBI Files, quoted in Thurlow, 1987, p. 238). Kriesche was a leader in the Bruderschaft, an SS underground movement which in the immediate post-war period had concerned itself with attempts to set up a network of foreign connections to ensure the preservation and propagation of the fascist 'idea'. These associations were worldwide and included connections with Mosley in Britain and also with the Arab League, the MSI, and Swiss, Spanish, Austrian, South American and French sympathizers who numbered among them the French fascist intellectual, Maurice Bardeche (Tauber, 1967).

Bardeche was responsible for one of the earliest expositions of revisionism, the attempt to rewrite history and distort the historical record by portraying Hitler and Nazi Germany in a more favourable light than has been the habit of traditional historians. This can be seen in his *Nurnberg ou la terre promise* (1948) (Lipstadt, 1994, pp. 50–1). It is very interesting to note that some of the ideas and techniques used by Bardeche are closely mirrored in Mosley's 1947 *The Alternative*. Mosley, like Bardeche, questions the evidence at Nuremberg and attempts to revitalize Nazi atrocities by insisting that all nations have been guilty of crimes in the past as a question of necessity. He conducts elaborate comparisons between the historical crimes of other nations such as the British government's policy in Ireland in the 1920s. So for Mosley Hitler's actions were not criminal and thus there was no question of culpability but merely of going 'a little too far'.

Certainly Mosley was one of the first revisionists to question the fairness of the Nuremberg trials and the quality of evidence presented, and to comment on the relativity of the evil of Nazi war crimes. There is no doubt that others were producing similar material at the same time and it is difficult to assess the source of the ideas at this point. Nevertheless, the relevance of Mosley's revisionism lies in its legacy and its relationship to other ideas current on the Continent at the same time. Indeed, Thurlow has argued that Mosley's early attempts at revisionism provide a link between the National Front, the British Movement and Mosley (Thurlow, 1987, p. 238).

A network of authors, publishers and distributors of fascist and neo-fascist materials was set up in this period which still exists today (see Ó Maoláin, 1987; Griffin, 1995). Mosley and his publishing company were part of this network exchanging the names and addresses of useful contacts and potential customers. Mosley did not only publish his own works but also produced work by other authors. Hans Ulrich Rudel was one of these. Rudel was a German air ace in the Luftwaffe and Nazi Germany's most decorated soldier. Together with Otto Skorzeny (SS colonel and Mussolini's rescuer in 1943) he was a leading figure in the Odessa network, the organization set up in the closing stages of the war to assist ex-SS members flee to South America by providing financial assistance to buy new identities and freedom from state harassment. Rudel played a large part in the re-homing in Paraguay of Josef Mengele – the Auschwitz 'Angel of Death' (Ó Maoláin, 1987, p. 131). This man returned to Germany in 1953 from self-imposed exile in Argentina, where he was an adviser to Peron, to run the Deutsche Reichspartei (DRP) – a Nazi revivalist party formed in 1949.

Mosley also published a journal of ideas and literary discussion entitled *The European* from 1953 until 1959, which was edited by his wife Diana, to publicize his ideas and those of like minded individuals. The contributors were mainly British but Mosley's idea of 'Europe-A-Nation', as has been pointed out, was far from original and its influence in fascist circles since the war has been pervasive. The ideology of UM was in the mainstream of fascist thinking in the post-war period and the European idea has provided a rallying point for many fascists old and new. Harris (1990, p. 27) considers that the idea of Europe 'is a key element in the continuity and coherence of post-war fascist thought and action'. Those who wrote for *The European* also contributed to other publications with similar themes.

The European had close links with Bardeche's magazine *Défense de l'Occident* and also with the literary journal *Nation Europa*. Mosley made regular contributions to *Nation Europa*, the last being in 1973. He also had articles published in the extreme right newspaper *Rivarol* and *Der Weg* (Buenos Aires). *Nation Europa* was based in Coburg and was set up in January 1951 and edited by Arthur Ehrhardt, ex-SA Youth leader and SS major who had been associated with the pre-war publishing house Voggenreiter-Verlag and was responsible for the translations of Liddell-Hart and F.C. Fuller. This publication was intended to provide a point of contact for those sympathetic to the cause and a forum for the international debate surrounding the ideas of 'Europe-A-Nation'. Like *The European* it claimed respectability and detachment from any involvement with activism. However, it has been described as 'a major organ of international fascism ... the contents of which seek to vindicate Nazism, support revision of the Holocaust history, show scarcely veiled approval of Nazi war crimes, propagate racialism, oppose immigrant labour and the science of genetics, and evince a shrouded antisemitism' (Barnes, 1981, pp. 38–9).

Many of the contributors were leading Nazis, fascists and neo-fascists and many have familiar names to those who take an interest in these matters, for example Hans Grimm, whom Hamm mentions in connection with the publishing networks. Grimm was a close associate of Skorzeny and a member of the Nazi literati. He was the author of *Volk ohne Raum* ('A people without space' – 1926) which contrasted the wide-open spaces of South Africa with Germany's cramped position in Europe and popularized the notion of *Lebensraum* in Germany. Amongst other contributors were Otto Strasser, brother of Gregor murdered in the Rohm Purge of 1934; Maurice Bardeche; Alfred Fabre-Luce, the French founder of the Association of *völkisch* Europeans in the 1930s, author of *Drieu la Rochelle, toujours amer* (1952) and a close friend of the Mosleys; Julius Evola; Filippo Anfuso of the MSI; Fabio Lonciari of Europa Unita and the MSI; Oswald Pirow, leading light in the South African New Order Movement; Karl Meissner, Reich Chairman of the German bloc and European Liaison Office; Carl Ernfried Carlberg; Adolf von Thadden; Theodor Souck, founder of SORBE – to name but a few. In 1973 Bracher was to conclude that for 'two decades Nation Europa has been engaged in establishing the continuity and the revitalisation of the Nationalist Socialist World of ideas ... so when Nazi slogans appeared on the walls of synagogues at the end of 1959 they were the old slogans and symbols' (Bracher, 1973, pp. 585–6).

In 1950 Mosley with Per Engdhal, leader of the Swedish fascist party Nysvenska Korelsen, was to become one of the founders of a new Europewide organization – The European Social Movement (ESM) – which was to be based in Sweden. In March he took part in discussions in Rome with representatives of the MSI, the Spanish Falange, the Bruderschaft and French nationalist-collaborationist politicians (Tauber, 1967,

p. 208). Here it was agreed to call a conference to take place the following autumn, again in Rome. At this conference were Nazi, fascist, neo-fascist and extreme-right delegates from France, England, Spain, Italy, Sweden, Denmark, Norway and Germany, and representatives from Belgium, Switzerland, Portugal, Albania and Romania (see Jaeger, 1960). The most prominent among the ten-man German delegation were Karl-Heinz Priester (former propaganda chief of the Hitler Youth) and Uwe Wehlen (counter-intelligence chief of the Bruderschaft). Others of note who attended were Anna Maria Mussolini (youngest daughter of the Duce) and Maurice Bardeche. The programme and ideas that were discussed in Rome were reminiscent of those that Mosley had professed in 1947. These included the notion of a 'third way' beyond fascism and democracy coupled with vehement anti-Bolshevism and, most importantly, European unity. Priester was to demand that they must 'destroy the barriers of parochial nationalism . . . to work and fight and sacrifice for a Nation Europa on a folkish, nationalist basis' (Tauber, 1967, p. 209).

The ESM was officially launched at the second European Congress in Malmo, Sweden, in May 1951. Among those present were Rudel, Bardeche, Engdhal and Lonciari. Mosley was expected but failed to attend and sent his apologies and Priester was denied a visa by the Swedish government. The congress elected Engdahl as president and Bardeche and Lonciari as vice-presidents. A European secretariat was set up at Trieste under the name of Centre Studi Europei which sent monthly bulletins in German, Italian, French and Swedish to the leaders of the national organizations involved. Attached to this was a press agency, Europa Unita, which supplied material for the neo-fascist press in Europe and overseas. A statement of the goals of the ESM was published entitled the Malmo Manifesto (Griffin, 1995, p. 342).

The organization also set up special contact offices in Madrid, Tangier and Buenos Aires and links were established with Skorzeny via a meeting in Madrid. Mosley appears to have distanced himself, at least publicly, from the ESM at this time due perhaps to the adverse publicity the movement was attracting. He was, however, heavily involved in the early stages of organization and maintained contacts with the movement and its members. The ESM held further conferences up until at least

1958 but it was continually subject to schism mainly due to ideological disputes about how much attention should be focused on 'racial' issues and whether they should work within the existing parliamentary framework or not. The moderates like Mosley and Bardeche, due to a question of pragmatism and strategy, had been inclined to play the race issue down, favouring the more democratic approach, whereas the extremists, such as Guy Amaudruz and Rene Binet, did not. They left to form a group with a more racially centred ideology and programme – the New European Order.

In the early 1960s, and after his failure in the 1959 election, Mosley was again to turn his attention to Europe. Evidence exists, in the form of a UM publicity leaflet, that he was preparing to chair a Great European Rally organized by Jefferey Hamm in November 1960 at the Seymore Hall. Those advertized to attend were Rudel and Giorgio Almirante (a member of Mussolini's cabinet and MSI). It is, though, uncertain whether this rally ever took place. Nevertheless, in 1961, Mosley was again at the centre of attempts to bring together diverse groups into a European Party. After a preliminary conference in Cologne, Mosley, together with Jean Thiriart (Jeune Europe), called an international conference to take place in Venice in March 1962 to propose a National Party of Europe. The conference was attended by members of the MSI who were the official hosts, Adolf von Thadden and a Belgian delegation. A document was signed which sets out its objectives and which Mosley rather grandly refers to as the Declaration of Venice (Mosley, 1968, pp. 435–7).

Although the ESM and the conference at Venice both appear to have been failures, like UM itself, in terms of mass support and gaining power or even forming a European political party, which was the aim, it would be a mistake to allow this to make us complacent. The contacts that were made in this period still endure today (Ó Maoláin, 1987). Roger Griffin (1991, p. 165) has pointed to the existence of an 'extensive web of linkages between nazi groups on both a Europe-wide and world-wide basis maintained through personal contacts'. I would therefore suggest that many of these contacts were in existence before the war but were re-established and strengthened as the war drew to its close. Mosley's ideas are very much in the mould of what many of his fellow travellers were saying in the early post-war period and this is far more than just coincidence. There are far- and new-right groups today whose ideas and personnel can be shown to have a direct lineage to these early attempts to ensure the survival of the fascist idea. I would name specifically GRECE (Barnes, 1980), CEDADE (Rodriguez, 1995), WUNS (Tauber, 1967) and Scorpion (Ó Maoláin) without delving too deep.

Thus although UM was a failure as a mass political party there is undoubtedly a legacy of some significance. In *The Alternative* we find evidence that Mosley's thought is clearly within the orthodoxy of post-war fascist and neo-fascist discourse. Griffin (1991, pp. 166–9) has provided a generic definition of neo-fascism and his model includes the categories of revisionist, new-right, third positionism and crypto-fascism, and although Griffin's intention is to separate out the different strands of neo-fascism, Mosley and UM ideology, it would seem, possess qualities pertinent to at least three, if not four, of his categories. Mosley's success was in the realm of ideas. His political philosophy was not only within the mainstream of post-war fascist thought, he was also a precursor, if not the originator, and guardian of some of its most important ideas and a party to some of the earliest attempts at forming the Fascist International which causes so much concern today. Mosley did his utmost to spread his ideas throughout Britain and Europe. Hence we cannot afford to dismiss UM as a failure for as Drieu La Rochelle pointed out in 1935: 'What has once been thought will be thought again. If it could have been, it can be again' (see Soucy, 1979, p. 18).

REFERENCES

Barker, M., *The New Racism* (London, 1981).
Barnes, I., 'The pedigree of GRECE (I and II)', *Patterns of Prejudice*, Vol. 14, Nos 3 and 4, July and October 1980.
Beckman, M., *The 43 Group* (London, 2nd edn, 1993).
Benewick, R., *The Fascist Movement in Britain* (London, 1969).
Bracher, K.D., *The German Dictatorship* (London, 1973).
Charnley, J., *Blackshirts and Roses* (London, 1990).
Cross, C., *The Fascists in Britain* (London, 1961).

Davison, L., 'Return of the man in black', in *John Bull*, Vol. 106, September 1956.
Foot, P., *Immigration and Race in British Politics* (London, 1965).
Griffin, R., *The Nature of Fascism* (London, 1991).
Griffin, R. (ed.), *Fascism* (Oxford, 1995).
Hamm, J., *Britain Awake* (London, undated).
Hamm, J., *Challenge the Old Gang* (London, undated).
Hamm, J., *Action Replay* (London, 1983).
Harris, G., *The Dark Side of Europe* (Edinburgh, 1990).
Holmes, C., *Anti-Semitism in British Society, 1876–1939* (London, 1979).
Hope, J., 'Reviving the Swastika: Mosley and the Union Movement', unpublished conference paper, Sheffield Hallam University, 1994.
Husbands, C., 'Why has there been no extreme right in Great Britain?' *LSE Magazine*, Vol. 4, No. 1, Spring 1992.
Jaeger, H. (ed.), *The Reappearance of the Swastika: Neo-Nazism and Fascist International* (London, 1960).
Layton-Henry, Z. *The Politics of Immigration* (Oxford, 1992).
Lewis, D.S., *Illusions of Grandeur* (Manchester, 1987).
Linehan, T.P., 'The British Union of Fascists in East London and South-West Essex, 1933–1940', unpublished PhD thesis, London University, 1992.
Lipstadt, D., *Denying the Holocaust* (London, 1994).
Lunn, K. and Thurlow, R. (eds), *British Fascism* (London, 1980).
Mosley, O., *The Greater Britain* (London, 1932).
Mosley, O., 'The World Alternative', in *Fascist Quarterly*, July 1936a.
Mosley, O., *Fascism: 100 Questions Asked and Answered* (London, 1936b).
Mosley, O., *My Answer* (Ramsbury, 2nd edn, 1946).
Mosley, O., *The Alternative* (Ramsbury, 1947a).
Mosley, O., *Union of Europe: Extension of Patriotism: Idea of Kinship* (Ramsbury, 1947b).
Mosley, O., 'A reply to Dr. Strasser', in *The European*, June 1954, Vol. 16.
Mosley, O., *My Life* (London, 1968).
Mullally, F., *Fascism Inside England* (London, 1946).
Ó Maoláin, C., *The Radical Right: A World Directory* (London, 1987).
Rodriguez, J.L., 'Neo-Nazism in Spain', *Patterns of Prejudice*, Vol. 29, No. 1, 1995.
Rose, L., 'Fascism in Britain', PRO HP45, unpublished survey, 1947.
Skidelsky, R., *Oswald Mosley* (London, 1990).
Solomos, J., *Race and Racism in Britain* (London, 2nd edn, 1993).
Soucy, R., *Fascist Intellectual: Drieu La Rochelle* (California, 1979).
Tauber, K.P., *Beyond Eagles and Swastika: German Nationalism since 1945, Volume 1* (Connecticut, 1967).
Thurlow, R., *Fascism in Britain* (Oxford, 1987).
Tyndall, J., *The Eleventh Hour* (London, 1988).
Walker, M., *The National Front* (London, 1977).
Weiner Library Bulletin, 1956, Vol. X, part 5–6.
Wilkinson, P., *The New Fascists* (London, 1981).

5 The Conservative Party, the British Extreme Right and the Problem of Political Space, 1967–83
Martin Durham

The formation of the National Front (NF) at the beginning of 1967 brought together much of the previously disunited extreme right in Britain. The League of Empire Loyalists, led by former Mosleyite A.K. Chesterton, regrouped with the British National Party (BNP) and with members of the Racial Preservation Society and, shortly after, another group, the Greater Britain Movement (GBM), dissolved to enable members to join the new organization. Both the BNP, led by Andrew Fountaine and John Bean, and the GBM, led by John Tyndall and Martin Webster, took the view that Chesterton had given too little attention to elections. Conversely, however, Chesterton and sections of the BNP were united in their initial reluctance to fuse with the Tyndall group which they saw as too overtly sympathetic to National Socialism for a credibly British nationalist movement. Tyndall's admission represented a suspension of this doubt but the continued exclusion of yet another organization, the National Socialist Movement (subsequently British Movement), was intended to ensure that whatever subterranean sympathies for Nazism existed in National Front circles should at least remain unexpressed in public.

From early on the NF demonstrated a propensity to internal dissension, Fountaine becoming involved in a bitter row as early as 1968, and in 1970 Chesterton himself was to leave the organization. His successor as Chairman, John O'Brien, would also leave in 1972, and while the defection of some leading members to the rival National Independence Party in the early 1970s would have little impact, a split in the mid-1970s, the National

Party, would be of greater importance. Fuelled in large part by claims from former Conservatives such as Roy Painter and Kingsley Read that the prominence of Tyndall and Webster was damaging the movement, the breakaway succeeded in gaining two council seats while the NF achieved none. But the National Party would fade away and it would be the NF that would remain the dominant force on the extreme right in the 1970s, capable of gaining 16 per cent of the vote in the West Bromwich by-election in 1973 and 119,000 votes in Greater London Council elections in 1977.

This was not to last. Where in October 1974, the NF's 90 general election candidates gained 113,844 votes (3.1 per cent per seat), in 1979 its 303 candidates gained 190,063 (1.3 per cent per seat). Neither NF votes or NF unity were to survive this débâcle. In November 1979 Fountaine, having failed to defeat Tyndall in a leadership contest, launched a rival group, the NF Constitutional Movement (NFCM). In January of the following year, a second breakaway, the British Democratic Party (BDP), emerged, and Tyndall himself resigned as chairman and, in June 1980, launched a further group, the New National Front. (For further discussion of the development of the British extreme right in the 1960s and 1970s, see Walker, 1977; Billig, 1978; Fielding, 1981; Taylor, 1982; Husbands, 1983; Thurlow, 1987.)

The NFCM and the BDP soon passed away and by the early 1990s the NF, weakened by yet another split, would have been overtaken by Tyndall's organization, now the British National Party, which even, briefly, gained a council seat. Whatever the future held for either grouping, the popular following for the extreme right of the 1970s had long since departed, and recent accounts have been concerned to explore the underlying factors in the NF's haemorrhage of support in the latter part of that decade. In part, debate has centred around the effect of Margaret Thatcher's much-publicized pronouncements in 1978 and 1979 on Britain being 'swamped' by alien cultures, with Eatwell arguing that the initial downturn in NF support was already in train before Thatcher's attempt to play the race card, while Husbands has noted that it was not until 1979 that many former NF voters decided to vote Conservative (Eatwell, 1992, pp. 186–7; Husbands, 1988, p. 76). This chapter, however, is less concerned with demarcating the role of the Conservative Party in detaching NF voters in the late 1970s than with its more long-term capacity to deprive the extreme right of viable political space. Where in Weimar Germany or modern-day France conservatives have been unable to retain the support of many of their voters, losing them to forces to their right, British Conservatism was to prove as great an obstacle to the National Front in the 1970s as it had been to the British Union of Fascists in the 1930s. To draw attention to this is not to say that the Conservative Party would under all circumstances present an insurmountable barrier to the extreme right, or that the NF's actual or potential voting base was solely made up of those who would otherwise vote Tory. But what we can do in focusing on the relationship between the extreme right and the Conservative Party is explore how in the period between the inception of the National Front and the immediate aftermath of Margaret Thatcher's 1979 election victory, developments within the Conservatives were central in the extreme right's rise – and fall.

This chapter will concentrate on three particular moments in the development of British Conservatism: firstly, as a result of three speeches on the issue in 1968, the emergence of Enoch Powell as a massively popular opponent of immigration; secondly, the crisis in the early 1970s within what was then the main grouping on the Tory right, the Monday Club; and thirdly, the rise of that blend of free market and traditionalist Conservatism – Thatcherism – that would come to power in 1979 and continue to deprive the extreme right of support in the years that followed. In exploring how the extreme right responded to these developments, we will be mainly concerned with the National Front and will pay particular attention to three of its leading figures, A.K. Chesterton, John Tyndall and Martin Webster, and the two publications with which they were associated, *Candour*, which supported the NF until Chesterton's resignation from the leadership in late 1970, and *Spearhead*, through which Tyndall (and, until 1980, Webster) expressed their views. However, both because the NF never brought together all of the forces on the British extreme right and because of the breakaway of rival groups after the 1979 general election, this account will not limit its focus to the National Front and, in particular, will examine how the different fragments of the NF responded to the first Thatcher government and the problems it posed for the future of the extreme right.

As Walker has noted, the coming together of different

extreme right groupings in the late 1960s was due in part to the impact of an article in 1966 by John Tyndall in which he argued that the recent electoral defeat of the Conservative Party was 'a boon to the Right', exposing it as a party 'of national surrender' no longer able to hold the support of patriotic voters (Walker, 1977, pp. 62–3; *Spearhead*, July 1966). It was, then, far from inappropriate that the infant organization's first opportunity of breakthrough should come from the pronouncements on immigration of a Conservative discontented at the direction of his party. While the first of Enoch Powell's 1968 speeches on immigration caused little stir, the second, in April of that year, led to an immense groundswell of support. Edward Heath was to dismiss Powell from the Tory Shadow Cabinet; the NF's response was, as might be expected, rather different. A.K. Chesterton was quoted in *The Times* as saying that Powell and the NF had similar views on the issue while *Spearhead* credited Powell with articulating 'what millions think and have been unable to say' (*The Times*, 24 April 1968; *Spearhead*, May–June 1968). Such was the response to Powell's views that he was to be credited with deciding the 1970 General Election and was to play a particularly significant part in opposing the entry of Ugandan Asians two years later, an occasion which was to add greatly to NF strength. During this period, *Spearhead* continued to express support for the figure who had given opposition to immigration such a popular appeal. In 1970 its cover was a photo of the Wolverhampton MP with the caption 'Bravo Enoch!' while in 1972 he featured once again, accompanied by the caption 'Immigration Common Market Northern Ireland Enoch Right; Tories Wrong' (*Spearhead*, June 1970, November 1972).

Despite this enthusiasm, the magazine was deeply critical of Powell's late arrival on the anti-immigration scene. In the editorial of the very issue that had greeted his April speech, Tyndall had noted that while such figures as Chesterton and Sir Oswald Mosley had long opposed immigration, nothing had 'been heard from Enoch Powell on the subject' until now. The following year, the magazine which had declared its 'debt to Powell' now declared that it was indebted to the left-wing writer, Paul Foot, for documenting how Powell had not opposed immigration until 1964 and had specifically declined to support anti-immigration activity in his own locality in the early 1960s.

This did not mean, *Spearhead* went on, that it did 'not welcome Powell's change of attitude. It simply means that we should not look to the politicians of the "establishment" to give a real lead in anything' (*Spearhead*, May–June 1968, September 1969).

Tardiness in opposing immigration was only one of the NF's criticisms of Powell. He believed repatriation should be voluntary, *Spearhead* complained in 1970, not compulsory. Furthermore, it noted, he had only recently come to oppose the Common Market, was a 'little Englander' rather than looking to the White Commonwealth and, while supporting law and order, did not oppose permissive legislation and did not stand for 'conservative moral values'. Perhaps most importantly, there was the problem of Powell's economics. Writing in the same issue, Tyndall argued that the Front should not be seen as akin to the Tory right, which was in fact more liberal than conservative. True conservatism, it was suggested, involved trade 'within a national framework, and in which the Guild System regulated business intercourse in the national and public interest'. Where Powell, Tyndall observed, had said 'I go on my knees and thank God for the gift of capitalism', for the NF, profit should be subordinated to national interest and a British economic area should be insulated from foreign competition (*Spearhead*, August 1970).

Returning to the question in 1973, Tyndall penned an open letter to Powell on the nation state. Powell, he noted, had declared that nationalism was central but had also described himself as a supporter of capitalism. Yet how could these be reconciled? The free market, free trade and a minimal state were not compatible with the defence of national sovereignty, and to see the ownership of wealth as an absolute right was to refuse to see what property really was – 'a form of custody deriving from the nation in return for services rendered and duties fulfilled'. But National Front objections to Powell in this area went further than the dispute between corporatism and the free market. For the NF, neither communism or large-scale immigration had occurred by chance but had been planned, part of a conscious design to destroy race and nation. Powell, the party paper *Britain First* claimed in 1975, had been a member of the Bilderberg Group, 'an internationalist financial-political body of vast ramifications run by, for and in the interests of International Capitalism' and this affiliation, it suggested, 'may go some way towards explaining his rather strange view – for a "Nationalist" – that Government should never protect British independence from international wheeler dealing' (*Spearhead*, September 1973; *Britain First*, September 1975). This attribution of sinister motives to Powell was not unique to the dissidents who were about to take *Britain First* out of the NF orbit in the ill-fated National Party breakaway. The suggestion of Powell as a participant in the international conspiracy had been alluded to in the past by both Martin Webster and another prominent figure, John Bean, the latter declaring in 1971: 'Perhaps his past attendance at secret meetings of the mysterious Bilderberg group . . . was not just naive curiosity, as some of us first believed' (*Spearhead*, June 1970, March 1971).

As early as the May 1968 issue of *Candour*, Chesterton had commented on Bilderberg and Powell (*Candour*, May 1968). He also shared with *Britain First* another criticism of Powell's role in British politics. The very fact that Powell was given such access to the media, Chesterton claimed in 1973, suggested that the establishment was using him as a safety-valve, an image repeated in *Britain First* when it suggested that while Powell had been 'useful to us' by arousing concern over such questions as immigration and the Common Market, he was 'in the last analysis a Tory safety-valve' (*Spearhead*, August 1973; *Britain First*, September 1975). There was another element, too, in the NF's criticism of Powell – the effect that Powellism was having on the NF itself. Commenting on Paul Foot's critique of Powell's inconsistencies, *Spearhead* had declared: 'At the risk of offending the many pro-Powell elements among our readership, we must agree' (*Spearhead*, September 1969). The NF was not the only racist organization in the country and, for several years after its inception, had to contend with rivals which it had not yet definitely outstripped. One such organization, the National Democratic Party, was involved in a 'Powell for Premier' campaign, an activity which was vitriolically attacked by Martin Webster in early 1970. Writing later in the year, Webster claimed that in spite 'of considerable criticism from many elements in the "Right Wing", this journal did not allow itself to be swept up in the hysteria of Powellism' (*Anti-Fascist Bulletin*, March–June 1971; *Spearhead*, February, June 1970).

But if *Spearhead* had been unwilling to follow Powell, it was not only within its readership or within rival groups that there were nationalists who were not. Writing in *Candour* in 1969, Chesterton had been particularly critical about what he saw as Powell's attempt to replace Edward Heath. Powell, he believed, was not to be trusted and he had had to decide to stop 'showing my friends newspaper photographs of N.F. demonstrations when I came across one which gave prominence to a placard demanding "Powell for Prime Minister".' For 'a movement devoted to restoring Britain's fortunes in the world' to call for a Little Englander as Prime Minister, he continued, 'would suggest that somebody within the National Front is under a misapprehension.' Speaking shortly after to the NF Annual General Meeting, Chesterton declared that to support Powell was to support the Tory party. One NF organizer, he told the assembled throng, was reported to have contrasted how many people had heard of Powell with how many had heard of Chesterton. 'Well, if it comes to that,' Chesterton went on, 'still more people have heard of the Beatles! If numbers be the criterion of the Portsmouth Branch, should it not leave politics alone and become a pop group?' Returning to the issue the following year, Chesterton denounced as opportunism the request from 'some of my colleagues' that *Candour* and he, as party leader, take 'a less uncompromising attitude towards Powellism'. Those NF members 'now attracted by Enoch Will-o'-the-Wisp', he hoped, would see sense (*Candour*, February, September 1969; July 1970). Such a view was more likely to inflame than persuade, and when soon after Chesterton's critics formed an Action Committee to demand his resignation as leader, he was criticized not only for his running of the organization but for his stance on Powell. 'Rightly or wrongly', the rebels claimed, 'he is respected by a huge majority of the British people and to attack him incurs the hostility of that majority' (Walker, 1977, p. 94).

Neither in the NF's leadership nor in its grassroots was there agreement about Powell. One local publication, *Britain First*, produced by the South London Area National Front in the late 1960s, carried in its first issue a two-page attack on Powell as a 'dyed in the wool Tory', accusing him of opposing capital punishment, belonging to the Bilderberg group, voting for homosexual law reform, opposing fluoridation, advocating *laissez faire* and misrepresenting the Conservative Party as a nationalist party (*Britain First*, November 1968). But while there was opposition to Powell among the NF rank and file, Chesterton was concerned by Powellism among both ordinary members and among those he termed his 'colleagues' and, according to Walker, he was successful in persuading Tyndall to withdraw an issue of *Spearhead* which he saw as promoting illusions in Powell (Walker, 1977, p. 124). Indeed, two issues of the magazine could have given grounds for such concern.

In June 1970, *Spearhead* declared that while it had been right to criticize Powell in the past he had 'rendered a tremendous service to Britain in his election speeches', particularly in what he had said about 'international conspiracy and the enemies within this country... So long as Enoch Powell keeps this up we will continue to say Bravo Enoch!' Elsewhere in the same issue, Martin Webster expressed a surprised belief that, through recent speeches challenging immigration figures and postulating the existence of a conspiracy, Powell was 'starting to produce the goods'. In making such speeches he had gone beyond anything he had said in the past and had put himself 'beyond the pale' of establishment politics. The onslaught Powell had experienced, Webster suggested, had apparently led him to realize the existence of a conspiracy and if he now understood the links between international finance and communism 'then he is on the right track' and 'deserves our support'. Two months later, the magazine described Powell's speeches of the previous two years as 'the most encouraging sign of a national awakening yet to appear' in mainstream politics. He must, it demanded, challenge Heath's policies, justifying 'the hope placed in him by millions of patriotic Britons... and earn the full support of this journal.' The magazine did warn that Powell might refuse to lead the fight against Heath. But in even raising the possibility of offering him 'full support', *Spearhead* was subordinating its criticisms of Powell in a whole number of areas (*Spearhead*, June, August 1970).

Powell's denunciation of immigration had undoubtedly helped the NF. One former local organizer was later to note how 'Powell's speeches gave our membership and morale a tremendous boost. Before Powell spoke, we were getting only cranks and perverts. After his speeches we started to attract, in a secret sort of way, the right-wing members of the Tory organizations.' Less vividly, Martin Webster, writing in the early 1970s, would note how Powell's speeches on immigration had had the effect of making the NF appear more respectable (Foot, 1969, p. 126; *Spearhead*, May 1973). But while Powellism had helped the Front emerge from the margins of the right, it was not without its costs. To the degree to which the NF supported Powell, it weakened the case for an independent alternative to the Tory right; to the degree to which it criticized him, it alienated those who eulogized the opponent of immigration, not only outside the organization, but within it.

Despite 'Powell for Premier' campaigns or the creation of other pro-Powell organizations, Powellism did not take on a stable or lasting organizational form. It was, however, of influence within one organization which had been in existence for some time and whose policy and potential the NF was forced to address in the early 1970s. This was the Monday Club which, since its creation in 1961 in protest at Harold Macmillan's policies towards white minority rule in Africa, had broadened out in policy to espouse a generalized critique of the direction of the party under Heath. Under the impact of an influx of Powell supporters, the Club became increasingly identified with opposition to immigration. It was, however, torn by disputes, both over Europe, on which it tried to avoid taking a stance, and concerning its attitude to the National Front, towards which many of its newer recruits felt a fellow-feeling somewhat greater than they felt to many within the Conservative Party itself. Once again, developments within conservatism presented the NF with opportunities, certainly the chance to gain recruits out of the Club, perhaps even the wielding of significant influence within it. But just as Powellism was potentially an alternative pole of attraction, so too was the Monday Club.

As with Powell, part of the problem concerned economics, as is particularly evident in an article in 1972 in which Tyndall put forward his views on a Monday Club publication, *State and Economy: Need for a Tory Rethink*. The pamphlet, he noted, supported unrestrained capitalism, and in calling for the reduction of state power was attempting to make a populist appeal. But the issue was not one of 'State Power versus the Small Man' but of choosing between state power and 'the power of gigantic business combines with international tentacles'. Big business, Tyndall argued, made it impossible for national governments to 'ensure work for their own labour force at fair wages' and the Monday Club, instead of recognizing the evil of allowing cheap foreign labour to 'undercut the labour of advanced countries', refused to defend British industry or British workers' right to work. Government should provide work, if necessary, and ensure national control of Britain's economy rather than allow it to be dominated by international finance. The Club, however, was seeking to revive a classical economic liberalism that had learnt nothing from the last hundred years (*Spearhead*, November 1972).

This was not the first critique of the Club to appear in *Spearhead*'s pages. In early 1970, it had published an article on a conference on subversion organized by the Club. Conference speakers, it noted, had attacked the National Council for Civil Liberties, the BBC and Penguin Books and accused communism of corrupting the West with pornography. It was, the article went on, 'a welcome sign that there is an awakening among at least some people in the Monday Club to the facts of life. But it is quite clear that a great deal more awakening is needed.' In particular, speakers had ignored the central importance of international finance capitalism in the world conspiracy. 'It is extremely difficult', *Spearhead* claimed, 'to believe that intelligent people in the Monday Club . . . are not aware of the dual subversive role of Money Power and Communism . . . We know very well that the Monday Club has to play a careful game. The many good friends we have among its rank-and-file members and junior officials are continually pointing out to us this fact.' To be coy in presenting the full picture was unacceptable and was not the only failing in 'this in some ways useful body'. But, the article concluded, 'perhaps we should be patient. At least the gentlemen of the Monday Club are learning. And for those who are prepared to learn there is always hope' (*Spearhead*, February 1970).

The following month the magazine returned to the theme of the Monday Club's failings in a two-page article. There had been, it suggested, a backlash against the Tories' 'continuous leftward trend', and this had mainly taken the form of the Monday Club, which was likely to exert more influence on the party. The Club had strengthened its position on immigration, was sound on law and order and attacked communism. But it did not attack international finance's links with communism, was weak on Rhodesia, South Africa and defence, and confused on Europe. As for economic policy, the verdict was mixed – the Club was for enterprise but it supported the *laissez faire* approach which had wrecked Britain's economic strength. The Club, then, did not really understand politics, and while it preferred 'the Union Jack to the Red Flag', was 'basically internationalist'. There were some promising figures who could come to the fore in the Club, and healthy elements in its rank and file, and it had 'a useful purpose as a rallying point and recruiting ground for people of patriotic inclinations'. It did not, however, 'serve as a reliable source of guidance for Britain's future' (*Spearhead*, March 1970).

Both at the time and since, there has been much speculation about the NF's intentions towards the Monday Club. In the late 1960s, two NFers were uncovered in the Conservative Party in Ilford, where they had been working with at least one Monday Club member, while in 1972 a leading Club figure, Roy Bramwell, addressed an NF meeting on immigration, the NF reportedly provided stewards for a Monday Club meeting on the same subject and one Club branch (West Middlesex) worked for the NF candidate in the Uxbridge by-election at the end of the year. The chairman of another branch (Essex) not only announced that Club members would probably support an NF candidate rather than a Conservative who was not opposed to immigration but also invited John Tyndall to address the branch. Tensions within the Club came to a head during the battle for its chairmanship in 1973, with supporters of the incumbent, Jonathan Guiness, arguing that his challenger, George K. Young, was attempting to bring about an extremist takeover of the Club and push it in the direction of compulsory repatriation and close cooperation with the NF. The West Middlesex branch was closed down, its secretary defecting to the NF, and Guiness's victory was followed by the dissolution of the Essex Club and a number of resignations and expulsions elsewhere, some, such as Roy Painter, joining the NF while others, such as Roy Bramwell, advocating a new party that would encompass both the Club and the NF (Walker, 1977, pp. 117–31; *Patterns of Prejudice*, July–August 1973). (For a recent discussion of Young and the Monday Club, see Dorrill and Ramsay, 1992, pp. 224–8, 362–4.)

Amidst claims of concerted infiltration, the National Front denied it had any such strategy. There had never been any intention, Webster claimed in 1973, of an NF takeover 'for the simple reason that the basic ideology motivating the Club is the defence of vested interest, defence of outdated and irrelevant 19th Century *laissez faire* capitalism.' Both of the candidates for the Club's chairmanship, he suggested, were economic reactionaries who supported the Common Market and regardless of how hard either beat 'the anti-Immigration drum', they would not support radical nationalist economics. As far as the NF was concerned, he suggested, 'the Monday Club is like a tree laden with over-ripe fruit which does not need to be picked. The defection of rank and file members of the Club into the NF is as inevitable as windfalls from an apple tree in Autumn' (*Spearhead*, May 1973).

As we have seen, this was not the first time the NF had expressed contempt for the organized Tory right. In part, this was because of cynicism as to the very purpose of the Club. Writing in 1969, Webster had claimed that he had 'no doubt that when the Monday Club was formed it was a genuinely radical group independent from the pressures of Tory Central Office.' However, he went on, it had been flooded by Tory loyalists and the very fact that Monday Club material was distributed through the Conservative Political Centre showed how little threat the Club posed. An anonymous article published two years later similarly declared the conviction that internationalists and liberals had been 'deliberately placed' in the Club to 'prevent it becoming a genuine right-wing movement'. The article went on to raise one of the NF's other objections to the Club. If the Monday Club did become 'a genuine right-wing popular movement', then it was possible 'for the Club and the NF to work as allies and friends and not as antagonists'. The real answer, however, remained the National Front and not a revitalized Conservatism (*Spearhead*, November 1969; April 1971).

At times, the NF was concerned that the temptations of working within the Monday Club would lose activists rather than gain them. In 1969, Martin Webster had criticized 'reactionaries on the fringe' of Worthing NF for believing that the Monday Club could save the soul of the Conservative Party. (Replying the following month, O.C. Gilbert, instrumental in founding Worthing NF and a long-time activist on the extreme right, objected strongly to Webster's attack, insisting that the

Monday Club was not right-wing enough but that the Conservative Party could 'be made far more right-wing by the infiltration tactics now operated by men like myself who for years have been members of the Conservative Party and who put over the policy of the NF at ward committee meetings and general meetings of their local Conservative associations': *Spearhead*, November, December 1969). If Webster had been critical of those who sought to infiltrate the Conservative right, in late 1970, A.K. Chesterton was even sharper on the question. 'Some weeks ago', he noted, 'a former branch organiser telephoned me to say that he had resigned from the N.F. in order better to infiltrate' the Monday Club. 'My reply, I fear, was a little terse . . . Anyway, how does one infiltrate a sea-mist?' (*Candour*, September 1970).

But, whatever the risks, the NF was inevitably drawn to attempting to directly influence the ferment within the Club. In April 1971, an anonymous article, 'Are Clubbers Waking Up?', rejected the claim that the National Front was behind revolt within the Monday Club but acknowledged that it probably was the case that 'an increasing number of Monday Club members are attending NF meetings and reading NF literature.' The NF was exerting a 'growing influence' and the right of the Monday Club now accepted compulsory repatriation was the right policy (*Spearhead*, April 1971). But more was involved than Monday Club members attending meetings of the NF. In 1973, the *Worthing Herald* reported claims that the local NF had 24 members in the local Conservative Association and that 'every Monday Club branch had been infiltrated by National Front members'. The source of this claim was Oliver Gilbert, the member whose enthusiasm for infiltration Webster had criticized several years earlier. As for Webster himself, in the same period, responding to reports that the Club membership list had been checked for NF infiltrators, he suggested that the information about who was in the NF could well have come from files stolen from the NF Head Office. Such a suggestion, of course, inadvertently implied that NF members could be found within the Club and, indeed, one journalist claimed that Webster had told him this was the case the previous year (*Worthing Herald*, 30 March 1973; *Spearhead*, May 1973; *Listener*, 28 December 1972).

Both the rise of Powellism and the key battles in the Monday

Club had passed by the time that the Conservative Party itself was to become the problem for an organization whose success needed the mainstream right to be alienating both its activists and its voters. The replacement of Heath as leader of the Conservative Party and the new leader's decisively right-wing pronouncements attracted surprisingly little attention from the NF. But the rise of Thatcherism posed two problems. The first was in widening the ideological divide between the Front and the Tory right. In both its calls for trade union reform and its attacks on the Labour government, Thatcherites insisted that the key issue was the defence of freedom. On the contrary, *Spearhead* claimed, 'the major threat today is not to liberty but to ordered society.' The 'most active Tory pressure group', the National Association for Freedom, it suggested, was more preoccupied with liberty than with order, more concerned with rights than with duties. The NF had been bitterly critical of both Powell and the Monday Club. The ascendancy of economic liberalism under the new leadership of the Conservative Party in the late 1970s was even more objectionable to it, and its antagonism was reciprocated. For organizations such as the National Association for Freedom, a party that did not champion the free market should not be seen as an ally but part of the collectivist enemy, and Tyndall, responding to Tory claims that the NF was socialist, declared that the Conservatives had donned liberalism's clothes while it was the National Front which championed 'the philosophy of the pre-liberalised British Right' (*Spearhead*, September, October 1977).

But more important than the ideological conflicts between the NF and the Tory right was the threat that Thatcherism posed to the extreme right's electoral reservoir. In early 1978, one NF writer noted how the Conservatives' opinion poll rating had risen following Mrs Thatcher's television claim that the Tory manifesto might include the ending of immigration. 'She knows full well', he claimed, 'that by vaguely aligning her party with the immigration problem, millions of ordinary and easily swayed voters' would support her. It was not only the Tories' immigration policy that concerned the NF, and shortly after the magazine also noted, for instance, how the Shadow Home Secretary, William Whitelaw, had promised a Tory crackdown on pornography while addressing a meeting of Mary Whitehouse's Viewers' and Listeners' Association. This would be good for votes, it suggested, but had there ever been 'such a crackdown during the years of Tory rule? There was not. More and more permissive legislation and an increasing tolerance of licence and decadence have been a feature of the last three decades of both Labour and Conservative rule' (*Spearhead*, March, June 1978).

The Conservatives' victory the following year was to hit the NF hard. In *Spearhead*'s view, 'the mood which swept the Tories back into office was one which looked to policies identified with the patriotic right.' But, it claimed, Mrs Thatcher had engaged in 'a gigantic confidence trick' and would not defend British industry or restore capital punishment or prevent the 'swamping' by immigration of which she had spoken. *National Front News* took a similar view, declaring on its front page that '"Thatcherism", as a hard-line new brand of Conservative policy ... stole votes from the National Front by stealing – or *appearing* to steal – NF policies.' Inside, the editorial asked: 'Where did half the expected National Front votes go in last May's General Election? To the Conservative Party – chasing promises about Immigration, Law and Order, and Rhodesia.' Faced with 'such a ghastly Labour Government', it went on, 'the prospect of getting even the slightest action on these issues proved too much of a temptation to the more gullible NF policy sympathisers among the electorate' (*Spearhead*, May–June 1979; *National Front News*, October 1979).

Tyndall, speaking to the NF AGM in October 1979, cited immigration, law and order and 'sorting out the unions' as examples of how 'the Conservatives pretended to adopt our policies – or at least part of them.' He had, he told members, seen 'this climate of opinion building before the election ... It seemed to me highly probable that the Tories would succeed in conning the voters with this hard-line "right-wing" stance' (*Spearhead*, November 1979). In 1978, indeed, *Spearhead* had predicted that the Conservatives probably would be elected and the following year it published Tyndall's speech to the NF's January 1979 AGM, warning of the risks of expecting too much from the impending vote. But the decisiveness of the Conservative victory and the shortfall in the NF vote could hardly have been predicted by the NF membership, many of whom would have been much more likely to believe the kind of rhetoric that had appeared in the Young National Front paper *Bulldog* in 1978 that 'the British people' had seen through the Tory pretence of opposing immigration and were going to vote National Front instead (*Spearhead*, June 1978, February 1979; *Bulldog*, August 1978).

In the aftermath of Conservative victory, all of the fragments of the NF believed that revival was possible. Both the British Democratic Party and the NF Constitutional Movement believed that the admission of Vietnamese refugees shortly after the election would discredit Conservative claims to be opposed to immigration (*Frontline News*, May 1980; *British News*, Winter 1982) but neither group, however, proved able not only to challenge Thatcherite hegemony but even to survive. (Indeed, a letter later came to light in which one activist defended his decision to 'work quietly through the Conservative Party' with the claim that 'more far-thinking Nationalists' had always seen the Constitutional Movement as 'a sort of "halfway house" between the Conservative Party Right and the outside Right': *Searchlight*, November 1983.) It was only the NF and the Tyndall group that would survive. How did they respond?

For the NF, opposition to *laissez faire* continued to be crucial in distinguishing themselves from the Tory right but the political divide was now deepened by a new radicalism. Previously, its new chairman, Andrew Brons, declared the NF had taken a pragmatic view of the ownership of industry, a view which had amounted to 'our tacit acceptance of Tory Capitalism, under which Big Business had dominance'. Now, however, he argued, it favoured small businesses and producers' cooperatives as against the concentration of wealth in the hands of a few. This did not mean, of course, that the NF had abandoned racialism for radicalism but rather that it sought to fuse the two and in the approach to the 1983 general election, it attacked the Conservatives not only over immigration (one article ending, 'DON'T BE FOOLED AGAIN – VOTE NATIONAL FRONT!') but over its economic policy and the presence of American bases on British soil (*National Front News*, July 1982; January, April 1983).

For Tyndall, in the final issue of *Spearhead* before the launch of the New National Front, the failure of the Monday Club and of Powellism had proved the impossibility of reforming the Conservative Party. With hindsight, however, he declared, 'we over-estimated what we could achieve in . . . the 1979 General

Election', thus creating 'the potential for widespread disillusionment and demoralisation'. The key lesson, he concluded, was not to rely on the illusion of an imminent breakthrough but to concentrate on recruiting an elite (*Spearhead*, May 1980). This rethinking on the eve of splitting from the NF was to go considerably further by the time that the New National Front, other ex-NFers and a section of British Movement were to come together in 1982 to form the British National Party. In a two-part article shortly after, Tyndall was to argue that both working inside the Conservative Party and outside it had failed. Since neither strategy had been proven, the new party, he suggested, should be flexible in its attitude to those still within the Conservative Party. If, for instance, Powell had created a new party at the beginning of the 1970s, the potential would have existed for the NF to convert a vastly bigger movement to 'hard-line' policies (*Spearhead*, October, November 1982).

In response to the débâcle of 1979, the NF had turned towards radicalism and Tyndall to a strategy towards 'patriotic, rightist sections' of the Conservative Party which he compared with the 'Nationalist revolutions of the past, which many of us may admire so greatly' (*Spearhead*, November 1982). But neither social radicalism nor a willingness to emulate National Socialism's relations to the German Nationalist Party were to prove successful. In the 1983 general election the NF's 60 candidates gained some 27,000 votes (1.1 per cent per seat) and the BNP's 54 candidates 14,611 (0.66 per cent per seat) (*National Front News*, July 1983; *Spearhead*, June 1983) and by the time of the next general election the NF would have split yet again while the BNP had recruited a handful of discontented Tories (*Searchlight*, August 1986; March 1987). Thatcherism would still dominate the political landscape, the divided forces of the extreme right not only grieviously weakened but unable to stand candidates.

In late 1976, *Spearhead*, commenting on events in Germany, had noted that the Christian Democrats had 'appeared to adopt ... the policies of the nationalist NPD – which, as a result, has shrunk to virtually nothing.' It was vital, it concluded, to expose attempts by the Tories to hijack NF policies (*Spearhead*, November 1976). But to anticipate a problem and to successfully resolve it was very different. Powellism had enabled the Front to move away from the political margins, and the ferment in the Monday Club in the early 1970s had given it new recruits and ended in the effective elimination of a political rival. In the late 1970s the NF was to face increasing difficulties and, ultimately, the disappointing results in the 1979 election were to plunge it into a downward spiral from which it has not recovered. In this demise, the nature of the political force which came to power in 1979 is particularly important. Powellism had signalled the existence of a political space that the NF sought to fill. But the resurgence of the Tory right in the late 1970s was to enable the Conservative Party to retake the political ground it had lost. In revitalizing a party that the NF sought to supplant, in popularizing a form of right-wing politics that emphasized the individual and the free market, and in taking stands, particularly on immigration and on Britain's role in the world, that appealed to potential NF voters, Thatcherism was to play a crucial role in the failure of the National Front.

REFERENCES

Billig, M., *Fascists* (London, 1978).
Dorrill, S. and Ramsay, R., *Smear. Wilson and the Secret State* (London, 1992).
Eatwell, R., 'Why has the Extreme Right failed in Britain?' in Hainsworth, P. (ed.), *The Extreme Right in Europe and the USA* (London, 1992).
Fielding, N., *The National Front* (London, 1981).
Foot, P., *The Rise of Enoch Powell* (Harmondsworth, 1969).
Husbands, C., *Racial Exclusionism and the City* (London, 1983).
Husbands, C., 'Extreme right-wing politics in Great Britain', *Western European Politics*, Vol. 11, No. 2, April 1988.
Taylor, S., *The National Front in English Politics* (London, 1982).
Thurlow, R., *Fascism in Britain* (Oxford, 1987).
Walker, M., *The National Front* (London, 1977).

6 The Esoteric Ideology of the National Front in the 1980s
Roger Eatwell

The National Front (NF) was created during 1967 by the amalgamation of several small groups. Earlier neo-fascist parties, like Mosley's Union Movement, had failed to attract significant and sustained electoral support in spite of potentially helpful issues, most notably primary immigration and growing social problems which had begun to emerge in some urban areas by the late 1950s. Indeed, Sir Oswald Mosley had retired from politics shortly before the NF was formed, believing that it was impossible for a radical insurgent group to gather widespread support – at least short of some catastrophic economic crisis (Eatwell, 1995a; Skidelsky, 1975; Thurlow, 1987).

The NF was meant to be different from earlier extremist groups like the Union Movement in several ways. In particular, it sought to play down overt links with fascism and to focus on more specific immediate issues, like opposition to European unity and the repatriation of immigrants (the latter increasingly became the main issue after the popular reception accorded to Conservative Enoch Powell's 'River of Blood' speech in 1968, which predicted serious racial violence in Britain). It also made no serious attempt to develop a relatively sophisticated ideology or programme – unlike Mosley, whose post-war writings were prolific and who sought to be recognized as a serious political thinker.

This populist aspect did not mean that the NF lacked a fascist side. Its two main personalities after 1970, John Tyndall and Martin Webster, had both been active in overtly fascist groups before the formation of the NF, in particular within the National Socialist Movement during the early 1960s. Although they claimed to have been converted to a more British form of nationalism, there is evidence that at the inner core of the party the basic ideology remained essentially fascist.

Certainly there was a continued addiction to anti-Semitic conspiracy theory on the part of several NF leaders and the claim that the Holocaust was the 'Hoax of the Century' circulated freely (Eatwell, 1991; Eatwell, 1995b). As a result, it has been argued that it is necessary to approach the National Front's ideology at two levels: an 'esoteric' one, which focuses on the concerns of the inner coterie, and an 'exoteric' one, which deals with the party's more popular propaganda, which was essentially populist – though some of the party's rank and file can undoubtedly be considered fascists too (Billig, 1978).

This mixed appeal quickly proved to have found a receptive audience, and the NF began to show signs of attracting a significant minority vote in local elections in towns like Bradford, Leicester, Wolverhampton and in parts of London, including the East End, Mosley's old British Union of Fascists' main hunting ground. As a result, during the 1970s many academic and journalistic commentators came to believe that the NF was set to become an important force in urban British politics (Husbands and England, 1979; Walker, 1978). This was especially true during 1972–3 and 1976–7, when the NF demonstrated that it had a notable following – sometimes attracting over 10 per cent of the vote, especially in local elections, though at West Bromwich in 1973 Webster managed to attract 16 per cent in a parliamentary by-election (Eatwell, 1995c; Husbands, 1983).

Tyndall and Webster, took these results as strong evidence that the NF was on the verge of a major electoral breakthrough – a view reinforced by the string of problems which afflicted the post-1974 Labour government and by the apparent weakness of the Conservative Party, which in 1975 had surprised itself by choosing Margaret Thatcher as leader. In the 1979 general election the NF put up 303 candidates – the largest number put forward by an insurgent party since Labour had made its breakthrough in the 1920s. The result was an unmitigated disaster: the candidates averaged only 1.3 per cent of the poll, little different from the perennial joke candidates. The NF quickly collapsed into warring factions and during the 1980s it largely disappeared into obscurity – from which it has never recovered.

A variety of reasons have been put forward to explain the electoral failure of the NF, including (Eatwell, 1992; Husbands,

1983; Messina, 1989; Miles, 1985; Reeves, 1983; Taylor, 1982; Thurlow, 1994):

(a) the civic and liberal nature of British political culture, which since 1945 has included 'anti-fascism' as part of national identity;

(b) a basically sound and respected political system, including first-past-the-post elections which tend to marginalize small parties;

(c) the role of the main parties, especially the Conservatives under Margaret Thatcher, in picking up the themes of opposition to further immigration and support for strong 'law and order' (which could be interpreted as a surrogate issue for controlling 'criminal' blacks);

(d) the absence of large economically deprived groups, or alienated subcultures – including the absence of a sizeable group of (ageing) former fascists to help keep the tradition alive;

(e) relatively effective state policy and policing, which especially at the higher levels balanced a commitment to free speech with the maintenance of public order (though at the lower levels there was some sympathy for racist views);

(f) the activities of anti-fascist groups in publicizing the Nazi past of Tyndall and Webster, and the hidden agenda within the party;

(g) an inability to gain favourable coverage in the media in an age in which politics was based on media campaigns rather than the mass meeting (though parts of the media – especially the Conservative popular press – at times set an agenda on issues like law and order and immigration which helped the NF).

These were undoubtedly important factors in explaining the NF's failure, but it is also vital to look at the leadership and very nature of the NF itself. The NF could not have broken the mould of British party politics during the 1970s – not least because traditional allegiance to the main parties was still too strong, and a revived Liberal Party was picking up protest votes (and some racist votes, for at the local level the party was sometimes perceived as hard on race). But the NF undoubtedly could have tapped a wider body of support during the 1970s if its leadership not been so clearly associated with the fascist tradition – and prone to schisms and errors of judgement about tactics (in particular, the decision to engage in large provocative marches). Moreover, during the 1980s, there is little doubt that splits within the leadership and the development by one wing of the NF of a most esoteric ideology contributed to its further demise as an electoral and street force in many areas of urban Britain. These developments during the 1980s also played a major part in the replacement of the NF by the British National Party (BNP) as the main force in urban racist politics – a virtually inconceivable development at the turn of the decade when Tyndall set up the BNP after breaking with the NF.

THE NF AFTER THE 1979 GENERAL ELECTION

The NF's activists

By late 1979 the NF had at most a few thousand members, mainly concentrated in parts of London, the Midlands and the North. Party membership had peaked at around 15,000 in 1973, and many of these members had not been very active. Overall, the party probably attracted somewhere between 60,000 and 70,000 members during the 1970s. Socially, most of these came from the lower middle class and working class. Although the activists were often relatively young, members were well represented in all age groups except the over 65s. Most members – and especially activists – were male.

Politically, there was a distinct split between the more conservative racists, and those whose views can be more truly considered fascist. Partly following these lines, there was also a split between those who disapproved of political violence and those willing to use force – though this split was in some ways more a question of age, with the NF's youngest supporters often having little time for electoral activity, especially the more long-run, mundane activities such as canvassing and the keeping of records. (It was largely in order to appease this latter side of the NF's membership that it took to running major street rallies in the 1970s, though the tactic was also designed to attract media coverage – a ploy which backfired as the resulting images mainly focused on violence.)

Even before 1979, the more conservative racists had begun to desert the Front. Many found the party's youth-oriented, activist side uncongenial. The increasingly nationalist line adopted by Margaret Thatcher after 1977 also made the Conservative Party a more attractive home than it had been under Edward Heath, who had expelled Powell from the Shadow Cabinet in 1968 over his 'River of Blood' speech, and who as Prime Minister after 1970 had taken Britain into the European Community and allowed into the country Uganda's expelled Asians – developments which undoubtedly encouraged divisions and breakaways from the Conservatives at the local level (Schoen, 1977; Seyd, 1972). After the 1979 general election defeat, this trend accelerated – though a few who joined the Conservative Party still retained a loyalty to the NF and were infiltrators rather than converts. By the mid-1980s, several former NF members had turned up as local and even parliamentary Conservative candidates, although the adverse publicity which this attracted from anti-fascist groups quickly led the Conservatives to be more vigilant about members' past activities. (On infiltration and the recycling of NF members see *Searchlight*, 1980– .)

A study of the local publications (surprisingly numerous, but usually irregular and poorly produced) put out by NF groups tends to indicate that initially the views of the remaining NF activists were in some ways unchanged from the 1970s. Leeds NF's *New Order* in August 1982 was made up of the usual staple fare of anti-immigrant politics and anti-Semitism: it also included the quote that '100 blockheads don't equal one man with common sense' from a certain 'A.H.' (Simple coded references to Hitler were common among the extremist fringe, most notably in the paramilitary group Column 88, its name being taken from 'Heil Hitler', and the fact that 'H' is the eighth letter of the alphabet.) *The Islington Press* (n.d. 1981) featured an article on the unlikely theme of 'The Jewish Connection in Ireland', while another article attacked John Lennnon as 'a product of a sick age . . . the candy floss society which has destroyed the youth of two continents.' Hostility to Jews and decadent capitalist society remained central themes for many of the party's hard core local activists.

The *Sussex Front*'s editorial in March 1983 welcomed the rise of the new SDP-Liberal Alliance, claiming it would 'free the electorate from their class consciousness', which would open the way for it to turn towards the real alternative – the NF. It also hoped that a victory by the Alliance, or a hung Parliament, would lead to the introduction of proportional representation, which would allow the NF to be rewarded with representation as well as just votes. However, falling membership and declining funds meant that after 1979 – and especially after the 1983 general election which resulted in a Conservative landslide – the NF contested far fewer elections than it had done in the 1970s, and members had to find other ways to fill their time.

Small-time social events to retain group loyalty became increasingly important. The *Sussex Front* in April 1981 proudly announced the guest appearance at a special social of Rat – 'the lead singer of the Brighton Punk Rock group H-Block. He really enjoyed himself, getting a "good Buzz" out of Organiser Harold Jane's home made wine.' This was sometimes linked to an attempt to attract a young following to replace the more ageing conservatives who had largely left the party – though the attempt to influence youth culture had begun in the 1970s. One aspect of this involved the encouragement, or creation, of local pop groups which preached a message of alienation and racial hatred. The best known of these bands was Skrewdriver, led by Ian Stuart Donaldson. A typical lyric included the refrain: 'Europe awake, for the white man's sake, Europe awake, before it's too late. Europe awake, Europe awake now'. There were also renewed attempts to recruit football supporters to the NF by a mixture of verbal attacks on black players, who were increasingly becoming a feature of the English game, and the prospect of violence. There were even 'League Tables' of which grounds offered the best prospects for action (Chelsea and Millwall tended to figure prominently). However, although some journalists and anti-fascists have portrayed such activity as part of a general NF strategy, much of it seems to have been organized at the local level. And some had nothing to do with the NF whatsoever: it was part of a more general alienated youth culture, which sometimes adopted the symbols of fascism as a badge of rejection from mainstream life rather than through any serious ideological conviction or organizational affiliation.

The decline in the electoral activities of the NF was also

linked to the growth of violence aimed at ethnic and political enemies. Advertisements in other issues of the *Sussex Front* included one for 'NF Brass Knuckles' – size 'large'. Another announced the formation of a video club which seems to have mainly rented violent films – such as *Mad Max* and *Escape from New York* (the latter was described as: 'New York has been turned into as prison camp where racial gangs are left to fight it out'). During the 1970s the British Movement (BM) had encouraged the recruitment of young people, even schoolchildren, and fomented violent attacks on non-whites. The British Movement had grown out of the overtly Nazi National Socialist Movement, led by Colin Jordan – though Jordan broke with the BM in the 1970s and it became led by the Holocaust-Denying, American Survivalist-influenced Martin McLaughlin. The BM's radical views meant that it was never seriously interested in fighting elections, and racial violence seems to have been seen as a way of encouraging race war – and thus radicalizing the political situation. Increasingly during the 1980s, elements in the Front adopted this tactic, and such attacks became almost commonplace in some areas. Although the main targets were the ethnic community, victims also sometimes included left-wingers, anti-fascists and homosexuals (Husbands, 1989; Thomson, 1988).

However, the exact relationship between this violence and the NF is unclear. Repeated studies show that most people who engage in racial attacks are not members of organized political right groups. The identikit picture of the racial assailant reveals that it is usually a male, mainly under 25 years of age, and often acting under the influence of drink; in general, they have low educational achievements, though they are not necessarily unemployed. This, of course, does not mean that they have not been influenced by extreme right propaganda and local culture. Although the NF's membership was relatively small by the late 1980s, its younger members clearly socialized with many non-members in pubs, at football matches and elsewhere. This unquestionably helped spread the message of hatred towards ethnic communities. Nevertheless, most of the NF leadership does not seem to have sought to encourage such attacks as part of a deliberate strategy. If such attacks were deliberately encouraged, therefore, the impetus almost certainly came from a lower level within the NF.

The NF's leadership

The leadership of the NF was badly divided even before the 1979 general election humiliation – not least over attitudes towards the party's own leadership. One faction can be termed the racial-populists, and often came from Conservative political backgrounds. They saw Tyndall and Webster as closet Nazis, who were an electoral liability. A second faction was more truly fascist; although views differed somewhat within this group it can be termed Strasserite in the sense that its members were often influenced by the belief that the leading Nazi Gregor Strasser (who was killed in the 1934 Night of the Long Knives) sought a form of fascism which appealed more directly to the working class, and which was hostile to the extreme leader-worship characterized by Hitler. Often overlapping these two positions, there was a group who disliked Tyndall and Webster on personal grounds: Tyndall was seen as too overbearing and pompous, while Webster was disliked more for his alleged predilection for members of his own sex.

By 1980, Tyndall shared this dislike of Webster, whom he largely blamed for the 1979 electoral disaster – though Webster in fact was a dedicated and relatively efficient organizer (Hill and Bell, 1987). In 1980 Tyndall seems to have sought to underline the fact that he was indispensable by leaving the party, setting up the New National Front. As well as his growing hostility to Webster, he also hoped that he would be able to reform the National Front on a more authoritarian basis, with the leader having to pay far less attention to irritating colleagues. If he saw the new party as a temporary manouevre, he made a terrible mistake for most of the other NF leaders had no desire to welcome him back. The split became permanent and by 1982 Tyndall had set up the BNP, which developed during the 1980s along much the same lines as the NF during the 1970s – though without ever appearing to make any significant electoral breakthrough. Indeed, a leading expert on British neo-fascism could write at the turn of the 1990s that it was only the NF that comes to the mind of the public whenever British racism or fascism is mentioned (Gable, 1991).

Webster initially retained his position in the party, but at the end of 1983 a coup removed him from the NF – a decision which led him to take legal action against the party for which he had worked effectively full time since 1969. In a series of circulars which he issued during 1984, Webster claimed that he had been pushed out by a group of young NF members who were seeking 'to achieve ends which are alien and obnoxious to *British* Nationalism by means which could bring danger and discredit to the party' (Webster circular, 4 May 1984: circulars in the possession of *Searchlight*). Webster claimed that he was driven out of the party because he objected to the emergence of a semi-clandestine organization among members, a group which was seeking to commit the party to a radically different public line. Webster's analysis glosses over the fact that he was personally disliked by some NF leaders, but he correctly identified the fact that in the period after 1979 many among the NF leadership had been overcome by ideological fervour, which reflected a widespread perception of the need for greater education of activists and for 'the development of a far more detailed and structured ideology' (*Nationalism Today*, No. 1, 1980).

During the early 1980s this led to a rather eclectic set of developments, with NF leaders turning to various sources for inspiration. Perhaps the most common early source was Strasserism. For instance, *Nationalism Today* (No. 22, 1984) damned capitalism for producing inequalities and alienation, and criticized Hitler for establishing a dictatorship and betraying early Nazism's early radicalism. During the 1984-5 miners' strike, the NF backed the workers – though not their Marxist leadership. Although the leadership was clearly divided and in some ways confused, it seemed to be pointing the party towards a radical appeal aimed at the working class in the hope that growing unemployment under the Conservative government, and divisions within the Labour Party were producing the conditions in which a significant change in political loyalties could take place.

Others, however, remained doubtful whether electoral success was at hand. The Falklands war had transformed Mrs Thatcher from the most unpopular Prime Minister since Gallup polls had begun into a conquering national hero. Although some of the aura quickly wore off, the Conservatives still managed to win a great election victory in 1983. More ominously for the NF, its 60 candidates in the general election attracted an average vote of only 1.1 per cent of the poll – even worse than in 1979. Although there were signs that the Labour Party was breaking up, there was no evidence whatsoever that outside a handful of inner-city areas the NF had any significant appeal to the working class. This further encouraged some of its leading members – especially a small but active and relatively well educated group – to turn towards more radical ideological approaches.

THE NEW ESOTERIC IDEOLOGY

The New Right and the French connection

One group became interested in the French *Nouvelle Droite* (ND), which had leapt to prominence in the French media during 1979, when significant publicity had been given to its ideas – especially those of its key theorist, Alain de Benoist (on the ND see Johnson, 1991; Sunic, 1990). In Britain, a central figure involved in disseminating New Right ideas was Michael Walker, a former NF London organizer, and by the mid-1980s a key figure in the theoretical journal *Scorpion*. The Number 10, 1986 issue included an article by Walker entitled 'Spotlight on the French New Right'. It also included an extended interview with de Benoist and another article on ND.

The line taken by those influenced by the New Right (not to be confused with the free-market Anglo-American New Right) was highly critical of the 1970s NF. *Scorpion* noted the old joke: 'Have you half a mind to join the National Front – that's all you need', and accepted that the party was theoretically unsophisticated and had fatally appealed to a mindless group of youngsters. In its place, the New Right supporters sought to promote a sophisticated and wide-ranging critique of liberal democracy, which was portrayed as a totalitarian society dominated by a consumerist and materialistic ethic – a line which owed much the the 1960s cult Marxist theorist, Herbert Marcuse. As such, America was seen as the great enemy rather than communism (*Scorpion*, No. 7, 1985). In place of consumer-totalitarianism, the New Right sought to create a (rather vaguely defined) society based on deep national roots, with a more spiritual sense of purpose which would end alienation at work. As such, it was particularly active in promoting ecological views.

Realizing that such ideas were highly radical, it did not seek to win elections in the short run. Rather, following the major Italian Marxist theorist Antonio Gramsci, it sought to achieve intellectual 'hegemony' – namely, its ideas were designed to win a war of position, to gain widespread support among the educated and influential groups.

A crucial aspect in this process was the portrayal of race and nationalism. The New Right believed that crude racism had in the past made it impossible for radical groups to attract any kind of intellectual following, or to achieve a wider sense of legitimacy. The New Right argued that there was no question of racial hierarchies, or superiority and inferiority. Rather the issue was one of difference: different peoples had different cultures, and each people had a right to its own national identity. The concept of who exactly constituted a people (the Catalans? the Cornish?) was left somewhat vague: indeed, in many ways the New Right was Europeanist rather than nationalist – it sought to defend what it saw as a threatened European culture. But the political implications of its views can clearly be seen in a section of NF publications by 1987-8.

National Front News (No. 93, 1987) proclaimed that 'the racialist position now adopted by the National Front is based on the Nationalist principle that self-rule and the preservation of racial and cultural identity is the inalienable right of all the peoples of the world.' This was more than just rhetoric. *National Front News* covers in the late 1980s even featured pictures of black separatists meeting NF activists, and perhaps most remarkably of all, pictures of and eulogies to Colonel Gadaffi, Ayatollah Khomeini and the American black separatist Louis Farrakhan (cover of *National Front News*, March 1988). Gadaffi's *Green Book* became one of the key recommended ideological books. Gadaffi's Libya was described by one leading young NF ideologue, Derek Holland, in his pamphlet *Ideas for the Future* (n.d. 1987?) as a model of 'direct, or people's democracy, in an actual and practical form'.

There may have been element of ulterior and hidden motives in these developments. The Arabs (and Farrakhan) were good anti-Semites – and a potential source of finance! Certainly the New Right's 'anti-anti-racism' (anti-racism was portrayed as creating a one-world culture) combined uneasily with occasional anti-Semitic references: thus *Scorpion* (No. 10, 1986) claimed that the Old Testament, with its claim that the Jews were the 'Chosen People', was a more racist book than *Mein Kampf* (on the continued anti-Semitism of the NF see Billig, 1988). Nevertheless, most of the NF leaders who argued this New Right 'differentialist' line were unquestionably sincere in their beliefs. The Arabs were seen as part of the heroic resistance to the world monoliths of capitalism and communism. There were also some similarities between the radical ideas of the NF and Islamic thought, particularly those focusing on the role of devotion, the community and of nature as something held in trust.

National Front News in August 1987 even managed to conclude that: 'There is a saying that "Black Is Beautiful". We agree!' It added:

> The negative racism which infected sections of the Front until recently was largely a product of British imperialism, which sought to justify the domination of other peoples' countries by portraying them as members of 'inferior' races who needed to be 'civilised' and turned into coloured Britons.... In complete contrast, the *racialist* position now adopted by the National Front is based on the Nationalist principle that self-rule and the preservation of racial and cultural identity is the inalienable right of all the peoples of the world, regardless of creed or colour.

The Political Soldiers and the Italian connection

By 1987–8, the faction in the National Front which controlled *National Front News* had been influenced by a second major source of esoteric inspiration. This group adopted a fanatical position, seeking to found an elite movement, with full membership only for the selected few who had undergone rigorous cadre training. This was not the NF of brainless football hooligans: indeed, *National Front News* in January 1988 specifically argued after yet another outbreak of violence that: 'Once again the modern day plague of football thuggery has hit Europe with some force, highlighted the more so because English football scum were present in large numbers.' The NF supporters of this radical-elitist position became known as the Political Soldiers, after the ideal-type, dedicated activist it sought to recruit. Its leaders in the late 1980s were young, and held college degrees: they included Holland, Nick Griffin and Patrick Harrington.

An important direct source of inspiration for this group came from a small number of members of the violent Italian Armed Revolutionary Nuclei (NAR), who had fled to London to escape arrest for alleged bombings in Italy after 1980. The key theorist for the Political Soldiers was Julius Evola (who was a key source of ideas for the New Right). Evola had never been a significant figure in Italian fascism during the interwar period; indeed, his pagan and mystical views had more in common with Nazism. But he published a prolific number of books and other works, and before his death in 1974 he had exerted a significant influence on sections of the Italian neo-fascist movement – including the Italian Social Movement (MSI), which had consistently polled 5–8 per cent of the vote in national elections since the 1940s, but which had a more submerged, violent side. (On Evola see Ferraresi, 1987; Ferraresi, 1988; for an overview of the MSI see Eatwell, 1995a.) It is not clear to what extent NF leaders were fully aware of Evola's thought, which is obscure and largely unavailable in English. Nevertheless, there are clear ideological links, even to the extent that this wing of the NF came to eulogize some of the relatively obscure European groups Evola admired, notably Corneliu Codreanu's Romanian Iron Guard – and the key theoretical journal of this group, *Rising*, clearly reflects Evola's influence.

Arguably the main concern of the Political Soldiers was the remodelling of human nature. In the words of *Rising* (No. 1, 1982?): 'We have reached the extreme degradation of the Western Man.' The pamphlet *Cadre* (n.d. 1986?) argued that the fundamental failure of the NF in the 1970s was a concentration on elections and rallies rather than building a 'new ethos', a fanatical, non-materialist, quasi-religious 'New Man'. In a form of Pol-Potism, it seems that this would have required the destruction of most urban life and rebirth in the countryside of a 'purer and freer life' (*Rising*, No. 3, 1983). In its more moderate form, such views appeared as a commitment to a greater concern with an ecologically pure, simple life.

There was a certain ambiguity as to whether this remodelling of human nature applied to society as a whole or more to an elite (Evola's thought was essentially elitist). There was also some ambiguity about the term 'Political Soldiers'. Evola was influenced by the German 'conservative revolutionaries', many of whom had fought in the First World War, and among whom military metaphors implied community or sacrifice as much as violence. Was the calling to join the Political Soldiers essentially spiritual, or violent? *Nationalism Today* argued that 'The true revolutionary rejects the coup d'état because it is likely to herald the replacement of one dictatorial instrument of government with another' (No. 43, 1988). Nevertheless, there seems little doubt that the Political Soldiers were willing to use violence to overthrow the system: their devotion was not simply to a new secular religion.

For instance, the pamphlet *Dealing with Repression and Internal Security* (n.d. 1986) offered the following advice on physical attacks: 'Dress for action' and carry everyday items such as 'a bunch of keys on a chain or a bottle of soft drink.' 'In the event of an attack, select and attempt to hospitalize at least one enemy.' An interest in fomenting violence also encouraged a growing interest in the situation in Northern Ireland, and the attempt to recruit members there. *National Front News* in July 1987 commented that: 'There is nowhere else in capitalist Europe where a proud and defiant nation is under such a threat of imminent destruction as in Northern Ireland. Nowhere else is popular rejection of the Establishment so complete. Nowhere else are a people faced with such a stark choice: *Seize power yourselves – or perish.*' It argued that as more and more people understood this, 'Ulster' would move into a truly revolutionary phase: 'Quite simply, National Revolution in Ulster is a real possibility, not just a slogan. Nowhere else in Europe is there at present such a chance to overthrow the Old System and to create a New Order where power, wealth and arms are in the hands of the people of an awakened nation.' Given the other contacts with Libya, it is hardly surprising that this led to growing intelligence surveillance of the NF.

THE BRITISH NATIONALISTS

The growth of New Right and Political Soldier views especially was greeted with derision in what became known as the Flag Group of the NF (after its main journal, *The Flag*). For instance, in the Flag Group's journal *Vanguard* (No. 15, 1988), the

Political Soldiers were denounced as a small group of 'intellectuals' for whom 'even some obscure Romanian had his moment of adulation' (a reference to the Iron Guard leader, Corneliu Codreanu, worshipped for his iron discipline – though some admired more his anti-Semitic views). The Flag Group included some who were relatively well educated, for example Andrew Brons, a college lecturer and the man who became leader of the Front in 1980, and Ian Anderson, who succeeded Brons as leader in 1984. But in general it was made up of the more working-class and lower middle-class side of the party, men such as the former NF youth leader, Joe Pearce. In the late 1980s this group had perhaps 2000 members, compared to the Political Soldiers, who numbered at most a few hundred.

The Flag Group's attack on the Political Soldiers did not mean that the group was nothing more than a continuation of the 1970s NF – minus Tyndall and Webster. It acknowledged that the 1970s NF had failed partly because it had attracted 'what can only be described as "elderly Tory ladies"' (*Vanguard*, No. 18, 1988). Brons argued in *Vanguard* (February 1987) that there had been a 'transformation of the party from a reactive [NB not reactionary] Party that knew exactly what it opposed but not what it stood for, to a Radical Racial Nationalist Party with a comprehensive ideology and a comprehensive policy'. This comment reflects the fact that the bulk of the Flag Group leadership should not be seen as extreme Conservatives, or simply populist. Indeed, there was often surprising criticism in Flag Group journals of the French Front National (FN), which was seen as having made a major electoral breakthrough in the 1980s at the expense of playing down serious ideology (though there were some who were clearly impressed by the 10–14 per cent of the vote which it gained in national elections after 1983). Most of the Flag Group leaders were radicals, but they were aware of the dangers of too openly acknowledging fascist roots. Some had been attracted by Strasserism in the 1970s and early 1980s, but by the mid-1980s – partly as a response to the alien influences on other factions in the NF – there was a new hunt for British ideological roots.

Among those welcomed to the NF pantheon were Robert Blatchford and William Morris, nationalist Labour pioneer, and proto-ecological nineteenth-century Marxist! Other British mentors included the early twentieth-century Catholic writers

Hilaire Belloc and G.K. Chesterton. As well as serving to stress British roots, these thinkers were also sometimes used to develop quite detailed ideological positions. So-called 'Distributism' serves as a good example. This was seen as having been developed by Belloc and Chesterton, and subsequently nurtured by the League of Empire Loyalists (whose leader, A.K. Chesterton, was G.K. Chesterton's cousin – and the first chairman of the NF in 1967). An article in the Flag Group's journal *Vanguard* (No. 18, 1988) argued that five features were required of a socio-economic system. Firstly, it should be inherently nationalistic. Secondly, it should eliminate harmful internal divisions. Thirdly, it should harmonize as much as possible individual self-advancement and the well-being of society as a whole. Fourthly, it should increase the sense of initiative and responsibility of the population. Finally, it should maximize individual liberty. Distributism, with its emphasis on cooperative ownership, was seen as unquestionably better than the other main system proposed by radical-nationalists, namely corporatism. For example, the division between employer and worker is constitutionalized in corporatism rather than eliminated. The worst aspect of socialism was claimed to be its central planning, the worst aspect of capitalism its class division. Corporatism managed to incorporate both. On the other hand, the best aspect of capitalism was its decentralization and encouragement of individual enterprise, the best aspect of socialism was the lack of a sense of exploitation. Distributism, it was claimed, offered both.

The split within the NF, and this focus on radical ideology even within the more mainstream group, meant that electoral activity was increasingly ignored. For the 1987 general election, no official NF candidates ran (one ran unofficially in Bristol, and won less than one per cent of the vote). Attention increasingly turned to infiltrating other groups, such as ecology ones, in an attempt to gain influence this way – and provide members with something to do. However, the mainstream wing of the NF had not entirely given up hopes of an electoral breakthrough. Whereas the Political Soldiers had effectively given up the parliamentary road to power, the Flag Group's ideological fervour had been designed more to differentiate the party from the Conservatives and to present a genuine alternative in terms of socioeconomic organization. As the Conservatives began to run into problems after the 1987 election – particularly over the poll tax – hopes of a new electoral breakthrough rose. The editorial of *The Flag* in October 1988 even described the party as 'on the edge of a significant breakthrough in Britain's political arena'.

The same month saw a *Dispatches* Channel 4 television documentary, sponsored by *Searchlight*, which clearly exposed the Political Soldiers' position. The group was already suffering from internal dissent and the failure to attract a significant number of members, and by 1990 it had effectively broken up. The Flag Group staggered on, but it too was harmed by the general divisions which plagued the NF during the 1980s – and by some of the antics of the Political Soldiers, which alienated many street activists who were confused about the exact structure and control of the NF. There was some talk of an amalgamation of the Flag Group and the BNP, which would have made sense organizationally – but the talks appear to have broken down over Tyndall's continued desire to be accorded virtual dictatorial control over any group he led. (On Tyndall's views at this time see his own journal *Spearhead* and Tyndall, 1988.) However, Tyndall had the last laugh, for the continued haemorrhage of NF members meant that by the early 1990s it was the BNP which was the main organization on the radical right.

CONCLUSION

Some anti-fascists claimed that the split within the NF was a deliberate ploy to pursue two strategies towards power, a more populist one and a more elitist or violent one (*Searchlight*, 1987–9; Gable, 1991). There were certainly some overlaps between the those who advocated various forms of esoteric ideology and the British Nationalists. It is important not to impose neat ideological divisions when the reality was often confused. The Political Soldiers were also aware of the need to present their ideas as part of the British tradition – just as the Flag Group were: thus they too stressed Distributism and forerunners like Belloc. However, there seems no doubt that most of the disputes were genuine. It is possible that the intelligence community, which was mainly interested in the NF for the light it threw on Irish and Libyan terrorism, may have encouraged factionalism, but it is not necessary to adopt a conspiratorial view for the divisions in the party ran deep.

It is important not to lose sight of the various reasons for the failure of the National Front which were listed in the introductory section of this chapter. They were undoubtedly the most important factors in the overall failure of the NF after 1967 not to break the mould of British politics – at precisely the time when other radical nationalist groups were beginning to burst on to the scene. But it is important too not to underplay factors relating specifically to aspects of the NF itself. One of the great strengths of Hitler in the rise of the Nazi Party was his ability to keep the various factions of the party together. The same point could be made of Le Pen after the formation of the highly diverse Front National in 1972. Both leaders also illustrate another point which is central to the theme in this chapter: namely, the ability to delineate policies which were seen by many people as central to national traditions. A vital aspect of the rise of insurgent radical groups is not simply the presence of 'political space' (Linz, 1976). It is also a question of legitimacy, the ability to present ideas as central to national traditions, the ability to attract others to cooperate or ally with radical groups. For all the barriers which exist to the emergence of a successful neo-fascist group along the lines of Le Pen's Front National, there has undoubtedly been more scope in Britain than has been realized. And a key answer for this failure must lie within the nature of these groups themselves.

REFERENCES

Billig, M., *Fascists* (London, 1978).
Billig, M., 'Rhetoric of the conspiracy: arguments in National Front propaganda', in *Patterns of Prejudice*, Vol. 2, 1988.
Eatwell, R., 'The Holocaust denial: a study in propaganda technique', in Cheles, L. et al. (eds), *Neo-Fascism in Western Europe* (London, 1991).
Eatwell, R., 'Why has the extreme right failed in Britain?', in Hainsworth, P. (ed.), *The Extreme Right in Europe and the USA* (London, 1992).
Eatwell, R., *Fascism. A History* (London, 1995a).
Eatwell, R., 'How to revise history (and influence people?), neo-fascist style', in Cheles, L. et al. (eds), *The Far Right in Europe* (London, 1995b).

Eatwell, R., 'Continuity and metamorphosis: British fascism 1945–1989', in Larsen, S. and Hatgvet, B. (eds), *Modern Europe after Fascism* (Princeton, 1995c).
Ferraresi, F., 'Julius Evola: tradition, reaction and the radical right', *European Journal of Sociology*, Vol. 1, 1987.
Ferraresi, F., 'The radical right in post-war Italy', *Politics and Society*, Vol. 1, 1988.
Gable, G., 'The far right in contemporary Britain', in Cheles, L. et al. (eds), *Neo-Fascism in Western Europe* (London, 1991).
Hill, R. with Bell, D., *The Other Face of Terror* (London, 1987).
Husbands, C. and England, J., 'The hidden support for racism', *New Statesman*, 11 May 1979.
Husbands, C., *Racial Exclusionism and the City* (London, 1983).
Husbands, C., 'Racial attacks: the persistence of racial vigilantism in British cities', in Kushner, A. and Lunn, K. (eds), *Traditions of Intolerance* (Manchester, 1989).
Johnson, D., 'The Nouvelle Droite', in Cheles, L. et al. (eds), *Neo-Fascism in Western Europe* (London, 1991).
Linz, J., 'Some notes toward a comparative study of fascism in sociological historical perspective', in Laqueur, W. (ed.), *Fascism: A Reader's Guide* (Harmondsworth, 1976).
Messina, A., *Race and Party Competitition in Britain* (Oxford, 1989).
Miles, R., *White Man's Country* (London, 1985).
Reeves, F., *British Racial Discourse* (Cambridge, 1983).
Schoen, D., *Enoch Powell and the Powellites* (London, 1977).
Seyd, P., 'Factionalism in the Conservative Party: the Monday Club', *Government and Opposition*, Vol. 4, 1972.
Skidelsky, R., *Oswald Mosley* (London, 1975).
Sunic, T., *Against Democracy and Equality: The European New Right* (New York).
Taylor, S., *The National Front in English Politics* (London, 1982).
Thomson, K., *Endless Pressure* (Harmondsworth, 1988).
Thurlow, R., *Fascism in Britain* (Oxford, 1987).
Thurlow, R., *The Secret State* (Oxford, 1994).
Tyndall, J., *The Eleventh Hour* (London, 1988).
Walker, M., *The National Front* (London, 1978).

7 Contemporary Fascism in the Local Arena: The British National Party and 'Rights for Whites'
Nigel Copsey

In September 1993 the British National Party (BNP) made its mark on British politics when its 'Rights for Whites' candidate was elected local councillor in the Millwall ward of Tower Hamlets in East London. The result of this local by-election immediately impressed on the national political scene precipitating a rather animated media response resonant with disapproving comment from leading politicians and public figures. The British Prime Minister, John Major, found it necessary to interrupt a Downing Street summit meeting with the Australian Prime Minister, Paul Keating, to express his displeasure. On the face of it, it seems unusual that an isolated victory by a fringe political party in a minor local borough election should produce such a heated response. Yet on closer reflection, it is easy to account for the resulting disquiet that the BNP's by-election victory engendered. Understandably the BNP's success was variously associated in the media with the rise of right-extremist organizations in Continental Europe (e.g. *Daily Mirror*, 18 September 1993, p. 6) where the BNP was seen to comply with a general European trend. Not surprisingly this tie-up with the BNP's European counterparts generated rather alarmist predictions of a fascist resurgence in Britain, especially considering that this was the first electoral victory for the extreme right in Britain since the 1970s. However, the British National Party seemingly belied this trend when it subsequently lost its council seat in Tower Hamlets in 1994. The failure of the BNP to establish a 'winning pattern' in Tower Hamlets suggests that its election victory the previous year may well have been, as one British daily put it, merely 'A nasty local difficulty' (*Daily Mail*, 18 September 1993, p. 8) rather than the harbinger of a historic national breakthrough.

Predictably, following a decade where the BNP had failed to win a single parliamentary or local council seat, it greeted its election success in Tower Hamlets in 1993 as 'A moment in history' (*Spearhead*, No. 296, October 1993, p. 2) where 'Thanks to Millwall, for the first time in over a decade we can say with confidence that a nationalist Government is definitely on the cards!' (*British Nationalist*, December 1993, p. 7). The Millwall result was certainly 'hyped up' by the BNP which subsequently pointed with self-satisfaction to a poll by the local *East London Advertiser* which claimed that more than 81 per cent of its telephone survey across the East End supported the BNP – this worked out at 3963 calls in the BNP's favour (*East London Advertiser*, 30 September 1993, p. 5). The British National Party further 'corroborated' its pretensions to power by citing a *Sunday Express* ICM poll which found that 81 per cent of the British electorate were 'concerned' about immigration and that 36 per cent were in favour of compulsory repatriation (see *British Nationalist*, December 1993, p. 7). These surveys suggest (as similar surveys in the 1960s and 1970s) that fascism in Britain does possess significant support potential when it is ostensibly mobilized around the immigration issue, as Eatwell (1992, pp. 180–2) has previously demonstrated.

The key qualification here is that this support potential exists where fascism is concealed from, but feeds off, indigenous racist culture. However it would be wrong to overstate this potential. There are numerous problems with the accuracy of surveys relating to, for instance, sample size and self-categorization. Having said that, opinion polls probably underestimate support for racist parties given that some people feel reluctant to openly express support for extremist parties. Clearly, measuring extreme right support in Britain is, as Eatwell admits, a problem (1992, p. 180). Nevertheless it still seems reasonable to conclude that the support potential for contemporary fascism in Britain when outwardly mobilized around the race issue is stronger than typically acknowledged. And this point takes us to the central theme of this chapter: why did the local electoral emergence of the BNP occur in Tower Hamlets in the early 1990s and could this localized success be translated into a national breakthrough given the potential reservoir of support for right-wing extremism?

AN OVERVIEW OF THE DEVELOPMENT OF THE BRITISH NATIONAL PARTY IN THE 1980s

The BNP under the tutelage of John Tyndall was launched in 1982 as an offshoot from the National Front. As far as the National Front was concerned, its former leader John Tyndall had concluded, by this point, that: 'Only the brand label remained: the winning product had gone' (Tyndall, 1988, p. 577). Perhaps in a vain attempt to rationalize his own failings, Tyndall pushed the blame for the failure of the National Front in the 1970s away from the Front's barely concealed fascism (which was a major electoral encumbrance) towards its alleged weak internal constitution and organizational structure. In 1980, when Tyndall resigned from his post as Chairman of the National Front, he ostensibly registered his disgust with the ill-disciplined internal situation within the Front. He insisted that this situation owed itself to an excessively liberal constitution alongside the infiltration of sexual degenerates and public clowns to positions of responsibility within the party. The real substance of the break, however, was a deep personal feud with Martin Webster (a fellow member of the National Front Directorate and National Activities Organizer) who had apparently enraged party members in the Midlands following homosexual activities (see Tyndall, 1988, pp. 246–7).

Interestingly, the departure of Tyndall and his acolytes from the NF in June 1980 was not intended to be permanent. When they set about the creation of the 'New National Front' in 1980, it was originally intended to reorganize and cleanse the NF, thereby acting as a force for its regeneration (see *Spearhead*, No. 140, June 1980, p. 18). But by 1982, Tyndall had resigned himself to the fact that he could no longer recapture the Front and the split was finalized. The BNP was subsequently launched on 7 April 1982 in London and was essentially an extension of the New National Front which had around 1200 followers, although it also brought together various elements from other fascist grouplets, such as the British Democratic Party, the British Movement and disaffected elements from the National Front.

By end of the 1970s Tyndall had become convinced that: 'A new movement was needed with an entirely different leadership structure, controlled by a single individual who would be vested with complete executive and policy-making powers'

(Tyndall, 1988, pp. 557–8). Rather unsurprisingly this supreme leadership position would be occupied by Tyndall himself (!): 'I knew realistically that among those available I was the only person who could undertake this task' (Tyndall, 1988, p. 558). In line with his critique of the weak internal structure of the NF, the BNP's constitution presented Tyndall with full executive power over party affairs, such as power of appointment, power to determine the BNP's political objectives and policy, as well as power to determine its organizational structure (see *Constitution of the British National Party*, November 1982, p. 3). Clearly this revisits the traditional, authoritarian 'leadership principle' cited in standard criterial definitions of fascism (e.g. Payne, 1980, p. 7) but that said, during any year Tyndall could, at least theoretically, be replaced by postal ballot provided that the challenger had served a term of least five years full party membership (section 4, point 1).

Although the BNP marks a significant departure from the National Front in terms of its organizational structure, ideologically, as Tyndall accepts, the BNP merely continued in the same vein: 'In most respects the National Front was basically sound. Its political objectives, as they stood, needed no alteration' (Tyndall, 1988, p. 248). This in reality meant a continuation of fascism. This point is open to debate and is of course contingent on how fascism is defined, but this exacting question lies beyond the scope of this particular chapter. However, elsewhere (see Copsey, 1994, pp. 101–8) I have endeavoured to show that the British National Party can be seen as fascist when Griffin's ideal-type of 'palingenetic ultra-nationalism' (see Griffin, 1991, pp. 26–55) is systematically applied to its ideology and political objectives.

During the 1980s the electoral strategy of the British National Party was consigned to an inferior position as greatest emphasis was placed on organizational development. Although the BNP contested 53 seats at the 1983 General Election, this was deemed essential so people could 'hear its name' – breaking the 50-seat barrier granted the BNP the right to one five-minute TV broadcast. This was apparently seen by over 13 million people, although even then, most people still continued to associate the far right with the 'brand' name 'National Front'. Indeed the BNP's impact on the 1983 general election was negligible: it averaged 1.3 per cent of total votes cast for its candidates, though this was more than the NF's even more derisory average of only 1.1 per cent (see *Spearhead*, No. 177, July 1983, pp. 11–13). Significantly, from 1983 the main focus of the BNP's political strategy was on long-term organizational development which largely accounts for its quasi-disappearance from electoral politics in the mid-to-late 1980s and also for its apparent 'failure' to make any impact at a local level until the 1990s.

In 1987, the BNP decided against contesting the general election choosing instead to divert funds to organizational advancement, in particular to opening a bookshop/HQ at Welling in Kent. Contesting the required 50 seats at the 1987 general election to qualify for a TV broadcast would have required £25,000 in deposit money alone which was prohibitively expensive for an organization with only around 1000 members, at the time smaller than both factions of the National Front. However, in eschewing significant electoral involvement (it did sporadically contest some local elections) the BNP came to be known as the 'no-to-elections' party (*Spearhead*, No. 264, February 1991, p. 14). This led to increasing lethargy and demoralization within the rank-and-file towards the end of the 1980s and apparent stagnation set in, especially after Tyndall had failed to amalgamate, under his control, the National Front Flag Group with the British National Party in 1987 (the negotiations collapsed when the National Front Flag Group refused to accept Tyndall as leader). In fact most BNP activities towards the end of the 1980s, probably undertaken by no more than 10 per cent of the membership, appeared to revolve around mundane paper sales, occasional rallies, leaflet distribution and circulation of the revisionist *Holocaust News*, rather than more 'inspiring' electoral involvement.

That the BNP did not break through at a local level in the 1980s should therefore be read in terms of a political strategy which deliberately refrained from fighting elections. The BNP's leadership insisted that a low vote undermined credibility and confidence, and drained scarce resources. Elections had been fought in the past to increase publicity but past experience of the 1983 general election had demonstrated that the probable returns in terms of recruitment were not worth the financial expense. Following its TV broadcast in 1983, the party was allegedly 'flooded' with enquiries (Tyndall, 1988, p. 580) but presumably a large proportion of those who displayed initial interest were unwilling to join the BNP following its miserable electoral performance (its membership did not rapidly expand). But for a party that professed to believe that 'ultimately, the ballot box is the only possible path open to British Nationalism to win political power' (Tyndall, 1988, pp. 581–2), at some point it would have to alter its priorities by necessity. Nevertheless in the short term, instead of concentrating resources on contesting local or parliamentary elections, stress had to be placed on developing party communications and ensuring the widest distribution of party literature in order to counter the hostility of the mass media as well as seeking to change the political climate through agenda-setting:

> We must build an alternative machinery of mass communication, and through it perform an educating role that will entirely change the climate in which political issues in Britain are judged. Only after that task has been largely accomplished should we attempt again to make a strong impact in parliamentary or local elections.
>
> (Tyndall, 1988, p. 583)

The strategic focus guiding BNP activity in 1980s is probably best interpreted as a formula for 'self-legitimation', as a way of challenging the de-legitimizing effect of the British media and its 'smear' campaigns, which had lethally damaged the Front in the 1970s at both national and local levels. On his experience with the National Front in the 1970s, Tyndall bitterly recollects:

> We had absolutely no means with which to fight back against the increasingly vicious media treatment to which we were being subjected. We possessed no mass-circulation newspaper of our own, nor any TV or radio channels. In the propaganda war we were like an army equipped with bows and arrows facing an adversary using heavy artillery, bombers, missiles and all the other accoutrements of modern fire-power. We had to rely simply on our own publications of very limited circulation, which were wholly inadequate to combat the barrage of lies and hate hurled at us by the establishment press and broadcasting networks...
>
> (Tyndall, 1988, p. 234)

Yet, despite directing most effort towards developing alternative communications, the fact remained that the British National

Party had still failed to develop its own mass-circulation newspaper by the end of the 1980s. Even in 1992 it appeared that the BNP's press had little more than 500 regular subscribers (see *At War With Society*, 1993, p. 23). To this day it consequently remains seriously vulnerable to media de-legitimization, especially when, strangely, its fascism is still barely concealed.

Nevertheless the British National Party had succeeded in displacing the National Front as the principal far-right grouping in Britain by 1989, though not necessarily through 'a series of well-organised rallies, marches and leaflet-drops' as one BNP activist claimed (see *Spearhead*, No. 259, September 1990, p. 11) but more likely as a consequence of destructive schism and ideological radicalization within the rival National Front which by 1989 had already split into two hostile camps and had virtually disintegrated. Although the BNP had reduced its susceptibility to internal division, had put itself on a sound financial footing and had modestly extended its range of literature, by 1990 it still needed to 'get its act together' and transform itself into a serious electoral force. As 1990 approached, Tyndall had no other choice but to accept that: '... during all these long years we cannot claim to have broken through to greatly increased public support' (*British Nationalist*, August/September 1989, p. 2). On reflection, he was compelled to accede to the depressing fact that the 1980s had been a disappointing decade for the British National Party. It may have replaced the National Front as the main actor on the extreme right, but it was still firmly entrenched in the political backwaters, marginalized and apparently stagnating on the very edges of British political life.

THE ELECTORAL EMERGENCE OF THE BNP IN TOWER HAMLETS

After nearly a decade of infrequent and unproductive election contests characterized by one to two per cent of the vote, the turning-point came in local elections in May 1990. In the Holy Trinity ward of Tower Hamlets (Globe Town), the BNP candidate and former NF activist Steve Smith polled 290 votes which was some 9.71 per cent of the poll, garnered from a relatively healthy 50 per cent turnout (*The British Eastender*, No. 1, May

1990, p. 2), an encouraging result seeing that as recently as 1988, in the Lansbury ward of Tower Hamlets the BNP had polled just 1.9 per cent of the vote. In July 1990 in a local by-election in the Park ward of Tower Hamlets, Smith proceeded to capture a very respectable 8.4 per cent of the vote. This was in an area that had apparently been free from fascist activity for a number of years (*British Nationalist*, August/September 1990, p. 7). At the 1992 general election, the BNP subsequently concentrated its efforts on the two East End constituencies of Bethnal Green and Stepney, and Bow and Poplar. In the former, the BNP's candidate Richard Edmonds polled 3.6 per cent of the vote, whereas party leader John Tyndall standing in Bow and Poplar polled 3 per cent. These results may seem unremarkable, but the BNP focused its efforts on carefully selected areas within the borough of Tower Hamlets and in these areas it claims to have polled over 10 per cent of the vote (*Spearhead*, No. 281, July 1992, p. 9). The degree to which the BNP had established itself as a significant electoral force in Tower Hamlets was confirmed in October 1992, when its candidate Barry Osborne captured 20 per cent of the vote in a local by-election in the Millwall ward. This significant gain was surpassed the following year, when the infamous BNP candidate Derek Beackon was elected local councillor for the Millwall ward with 34 per cent of the vote (1480 votes) in September 1993.

Foremost impressions of what proved the catalyst for the BNP's electoral breakthrough in Tower Hamlets chiefly focused on the alleged contribution made by the ruling Liberal Democrats in the Borough, the so-called 'Liberal Focus' group, who by supposedly politicizing race at a local level created legitimate political space for the racist BNP. In preparing fertile ground for the BNP's racial populism, it was argued that the ruling Liberal Democrats paved the way for Beackon's electoral victory. Liberal Focus, as one commentator put it, had '... sown the seeds of the electoral harvest reaped by Britain's foremost Neo-Nazi party' (*New Statesman and Society*, 24 September 1993, p. 33). However, amid the political in-fighting that followed, counter-allegations were directed at the local Labour Party which confused the culpability: the Labour Party, by circulating false canvass returns, had apparently 'talked up' the BNP's support during the 1993 by-election which gave the BNP added electoral credibility. Other commentators saw the local electoral emergence of the BNP as the rather inevitable outcome of widespread social deprivation, political alienation, crime and unemployment (see *The Guardian*, 18 September 1993, p. 26).

More perceptively David Cesarani argued that the BNP's rise owed itself to a 'belligerent and deeply objectionable defence of community' (see *The Guardian*, 21 September 1993, p. 20). The same interpretation was repeated by Sivanandan who maintained that white communities in the East End were dying: '... and what the BNP offered them is the chance to found an imagined community out of their bloodstock racism' with racism being 'the comfort of the last resort' (*New Statesman and Society*, 15 October 1993, p. 16). But unfortunately, few have bothered to pay serious attention to the restructured activities and tactics of the BNP as a trigger factor in its rise to local prominence. In particular, it should not be overlooked that through launching its 'Rights for Whites' campaign, the British National Party did skilfully succeed in constructing and establishing itself as a *legitimate* defender of the white community in Tower Hamlets.

Characteristic of many urban areas in Britain, Tower Hamlets has undergone deindustrialization (with the decline of traditional manufacturing and dock-related industries). The borough remains one of the poorest in Britain. The unemployment rate is 20 per cent, and over 80 per cent of housing is council owned. A high proportion of this housing stock, moreover, is in poor condition, a plight further aggravated by severe problems of overcrowding and homelessness with 22,000 households on the housing transfer or waiting list with close to 800 families on the homeless register. Of those households deemed homeless in 1992/3, 78 per cent were from ethnic minorities who make up one-third of the 170, 000 inhabitants who reside in Tower Hamlets, 75 per cent of whom are Bangladeshi who form the largest single ethnic minority group in any London borough. The white population is ageing whilst the ethnic minority population is growing rapidly. Physically, the appearance of the borough is quite unique. In the midst of decaying traditional East End areas such as Spitalfields, Wapping, Bow, Stepney Bethnal Green and Poplar lies the ultra-modern 'Docklands' development, which contains the prestigious Canary Wharf site. This development is said to form an 'enclave' to which most gentrification is restricted (see Lowndes and Stoker, 1992), but by providing such a sharply evident contrast the Docklands development cannot help but reinforce an acute sense of relative socio-economic deprivation, parochialism and introspection. Seen from this side of the divide, not surprisingly, as one journalist has written, each impoverished neighbourhood 'constitutes a kind of socio-spatial prison' (*The Guardian*, 27 October 1993, p. 12).

This austere confinement has arguably engendered a localized 'crisis of community consciousness' as traditional sources of social solidarity have been dissolved by uncompromising structural change (deindustrialization, ethnic minority concentration, insensitive urban redevelopment) which has contrived to produce a peculiarly 'anomic' environment conducive to racist political mobilization. This structural change has helped precipitate a racist backlash where fragmentation of long-established and historically inward-looking communities, such as Millwall, has become the major fear. Preliminary studies of extreme right support in the area show that a key factor in determining BNP support is length of time resident in the Borough. An ICM poll, commissioned by Tower Hamlets Independent News Service (THINK) in Millwall in March 1994, found that BNP support came equally from male and female residents, but 60 per cent of BNP voters had lived in the area for 21 years or more, although these only make up 30 per cent of the population (THINK Press Release, 31 March 1994, p. 4). Undeniably, the specific socio-economic configuration that exists in Tower Hamlets has been the overarching factor in the BNP's local electoral success, but having said that, the stigma that is attached to fascism should also be considered. The fact that the British National Party obtained the requisite political legitimacy to constitute an acceptable political actor in the local arena must also be of supreme importance especially considering that, on the one hand, there is the appalling Nazi legacy to contend with, while on the other hand, there is the additional obstacle that fascism appears unpatriotic and foreign, an 'obscenity' that 'decent British folk' fought against during the Second World War (see Kushner, 1994, p. 33).

For all the resilience of this barrier, it remains that the BNP overcame this 'acceptability obstruction' and local legitimation of the British National Party in Tower Hamlets did take place. Significantly, this legitimation came about in successive stages as a direct consequence of an ongoing interchange between external and internal dynamics. Externally, it resulted from the progressive creation of legitimate political space, in the main as a result of the ruling Liberal Democrats pandering to white voter hostility against the local ethnic minority community. Internally, it resulted from the BNP's enterprising 'Rights for Whites' campaign which recurringly fed off the racial prejudice encouraged to grow by this institutionalized racism. The manipulation of race as a political issue at the institutional level appears to have been carried out for purely electoral reasons (as white voters provided the majority of support for the Liberal Democrats in 1986) rather than as a result of deep-rooted racial prejudice. This use of the 'race card', however, was not a recent development.

After gaining power following local elections in 1986, the new local Liberal administration made a series of controversial policy decisions that employed 'covert racism' merely for political gain. This involved politicizing race behind the thinly disguised veil of a local housing crisis which had become a source of acute racial friction in 1984 when tenants associations complained of preferential treatment for Bangladeshis (see *Searchlight*, No. 110, August 1984, p. 17). In April 1987 the council issued eviction notices to over 90 Bangladeshi families living in bed and breakfast accommodation because these families had 'rendered themselves intentionally homeless' (see Fekete, 1990, p. 73). The Council also introduced a 'Sons and Daughters' housing scheme in 1987 which was intended to allow sons and daughters of local residents to be rehoused within Tower Hamlets close to their parents. This disproportionately favoured white applicants by using residency points based on the length of parental residence in the borough. Election literature circulated in 1990 by Liberal Focus played on the 'Sons and Daughters' theme and generated the impression that the Liberal Democrats were in favour of giving 'local', i.e. white, residents preferential treatment in housing allocation. Moreover, a bogus, supposedly Labour leaflet was also distributed by the Liberal Democrats during the May 1990 local elections. This 'Labour News' leaflet included the following declaration:

HOMES FOR LOCALS – RACIST! SAYS LABOUR
In the last 4 years Bangladeshi people in Tower Hamlets have been discriminated against by Liberal's racist housing policies, like the Sons and Daughters scheme and their decision not to house homeless families because they left homes abroad. Labour will scrap these policies and see that Bangladeshis are treated fairly.
(*Political Speech and Race Relations in a Liberal Democracy*, 1993, p. 30)

The election literature circulated by the Liberal Democrats at the local elections in 1990, the point at which the BNP first made its electoral gains in Tower Hamlets, did 'covertly' exploit race for political gain. By employing racism in a 'bid for votes', the Liberal Democrats only helped to encourage and endorse white hostility towards ethnic minorities thereby allowing the British National Party to enter the orbit of legitimate political space.

Yet it was also significant that the BNP was able to project itself into this space. Advantageously for the BNP, in February 1990 a white schoolboy, John Stoner, was attacked and stabbed in Morpeth School in Bethnal Green by a group of Asian children in an incident which the local police and press pronounced 'racist'. A march by around 300 white residents, with no 'clear' connection with the BNP (the foster parents and grandfather subsequently denied any association) was joined by around 50 activists from the local Tower Hamlets and Hackney Branch of the British National Party, which includes many former NF members. Interestingly, this initiative was not orchestrated by the leadership of the party who, on the very same day of the march, were holding a rally in Milton Keynes (*British Nationalist*, March 1990, p. 8). Rather, it was a grassroots initiative whereby local BNP activists became involved in spontaneous local protest and then more systematically set about organizing a deceptive 'Rights for Whites' campaign.

At the outset, the British National Party misleadingly endeavoured to use this campaign as a 'false front' which on at least one occasion hoodwinked the local *East London Advertiser* (9 March 1990, p. 1) which (mis)reported that: 'A right-wing group calling itself the "Rights for Whites Campaign" ... has been leafleting the Borough.' Indeed in an early 'Rights for Whites' leaflet distributed by the British National Party, it was not immediately obvious that the campaign was sponsored by the BNP. On one particular leaflet, supporters of the 'Rights for Whites Campaign' were instructed to write to a post office box in East London. This belonged to David Ettridge, a local BNP activist (and former member of the NF) who contested St James ward in Tower Hamlets at the local elections in 1990. However, this devious scheme was short-lived: during a 'Rights for Whites' march through Bethnal Green in March 1990, the BNP handed out further leaflets, distributed stickers and allegedly 'sold hundreds of copies' of *British Nationalist* to local residents (see *British Nationalist*, April 1990, p. 8) and from this point, the BNP clearly exposed itself as the architect of the 'Rights for Whites' campaign.

Where during the 1980s the BNP had purposely refrained from heavy involvement in local electoral arenas, the development of this 'Rights for Whites' campaign can be seen as an important and decisive strategic deviation away from established practice. Perhaps the saving grace for the BNP was that this campaign appears to have been set in motion by local activists rather than prompted by a faltering leadership who, at the time, still seemed reluctant to make a heavy investment in local electoral politics. With its initial electoral gains, however, the leadership quickly adjusted its convictions and was soon appealing to its activists to ensure: '... that the BNP establish and entrench itself deeply, firmly and solidly within white communities all over the country, just as we are doing with some success in the East End of London' (*Spearhead*, No. 281, July 1992, p. 9). Throughout the 1980s the leadership had promised to invest in electoral activity at a 'later date'; now in the 1990s it could hardly prevaricate when such a debilitating mood of apathy was emaciating the party. Now was the appropriate time to make '... the first tentative steps towards a larger commitment of manpower and money to electoral activities' (*British Nationalist*, May/June 1990, p. 8). Consequently from 1990 the BNP embraced a new political strategy (incidentally, the National Front had developed a similar 'Community Action' strategy in the 1980s) which basically involved sinking local community roots through 'public-spirited' activity. The aim was to neutralize the Nazi 'smear' by local contact and to construct some semblance of local political legitimacy by clearly substantiating a social conscience. Thus the quasi-liberal discourse of 'Defend Rights for Whites' with accompanying appeals for 'Justice' identified the BNP with a 'public-spirited' campaign while its rational, 'liberal' discourse seemingly divorced the BNP from the irrational, injudicious extremism of fascism.

By attaching itself to local protest in 1990, and then embedding itself within the local white community through its 'Rights for Whites' campaign, the BNP emerged as a legitimate champion of local white residents in Tower Hamlets and therefore, in part, *brought itself* into the local mainstream. Perhaps the BNP also benefited, in terms of its legitimation, from an above average extreme-right residue in the area considering that the National Front had polled 21.1 per cent of the vote in Millwall in 1978 (*CARF*, No. 1, February/March 1991, p. 4). But this should not be overstated – the Front's support in the area had collapsed by 1982. Productively the BNP's propaganda from 1990 onwards sought to deprive the covert racism of Liberal Focus of any credibility by claiming that, in practice, the ruling Liberal Democrats actually put ethnic minority groups first in housing provision, education, jobs and welfare. The BNP's message was 'reasonable' and 'unextreme': the rights of white residents had to be defended in the areas which affect everyday lives, as one BNP activist implored: 'We must stop talking just about what we like to talk about and start talking about the things local people are crying out to hear' (*Spearhead*, No. 281, July 1992, p. 9). Indicative of this approach the BNP picketed the Town Hall against the closure of a local nursery in the run up to the Park ward by-election in July 1990. Apparently local mothers welcomed the BNP which was clearly no longer an 'outsider' and chanted its slogan 'Rights for Whites' (see *British Nationalist*, August/September 1990, p. 7).

Fortunately for the BNP, at the institutional level between 1990 and 1993, the ruling Liberal Democrats *repetitively* manipulated the race issue. This ensured that the local agenda was dominated by race which 'kept the kettle boiling' for the BNP's 'Rights for Whites' campaign: on 8 November 1991 the back page of the *East London Advertiser* (circulation: 24,000) reported that a top Liberal Democrat councillor was going to Bangladesh to tell them: 'We've got no room left for immigrants'; at the 1992 general election, the same councillor distributed a leaflet boasting that he had '... fought and spoken up for homes for local youngsters (and had been called 'racist' as a result...)' thereby implying that he had been a victim of anti-white 'political correctness' (see *Political Speech and Race Relations in a Liberal Democracy*, 1993, pp. 36–40). During the same election campaign, a Liberal Democrat councillor refused to lower the Union Jack from council offices in Globe Town. This councillor (who had been present on the Stoner protest march) earned the approval of the *East London Advertiser* which printed a full page Union Jack (10 April 1992, p. 24) for readers to cut out and display despite the fact that the Union Jack had become a well-known symbol of the BNP. Three incriminating leaflets were distributed by the Liberal Democrats at the 1992 Millwall by-election (where Osborne polled 20 per cent) which again manipulated the race issue. One suggested that the Liberal Democrats favoured the resident white community, another attacked Labour's 'positive discrimination' policy, while a further leaflet claimed the local Labour Party had said 'NO to Island Homes for Island People' (see *Political Speech and Race Relations in a Liberal Democracy*, 1993, pp. 36–40). The combined message: the Liberal Democrats favour the white community, i.e. the 'real' Islanders, whereas Labour favours Bangladeshi immigrants.

The litany continues: at the 1993 Millwall by-election (where Beackon was elected), a leaflet was distributed by Liberal Focus describing how Labour councillors had tried to donate £30,000 to Bangladeshi flood relief and had given the Bangladeshi Youth Movement £175,000. This particular leaflet became known as the 'Toilet Leaflet' – it featured a toilet with an arrow pointing down to it, above which was written: 'HOW LABOUR SPENDS YOUR MONEY'. Even following the BNP's by-election victory, another suspect leaflet was distributed by the local Liberal Democrats which carried an illustration of a black boxer. Above this illustration it read: 'Mrs X, a 74 year old decorated during the war, lives alone on the fifth floor of a block on, possibly, Wapping's most dangerous estate' (see *Political Speech and Race Relations in a Liberal Democracy*, 1993, pp. 40–49). The coded implication: ethnic minorities were responsible for crime.

The point that the Liberal Democrats in Tower Hamlets were responsible for opening up legitimate political space for the British National Party seems beyond doubt, though, to be even handed, one should not exonerate the Labour Party. Two Labour leaflets circulated during the 1993 Millwall by-election seemed to imply that Labour supported a housing policy that favoured white residents while also providing false canvass returns that further elevated the BNP's electoral credibility. It seems that Labour 'talked up' the BNP vote in order to steal votes from the Liberal Democrats whose support they 'talked down' while also trying to persuade indecisive Labour supporters to cast their vote or else risk a BNP victory. However, despite Labour's contribution, prime responsibility for encouraging and setting a political climate in which white voters believed that their antagonism towards the ethnic minority community was justified still rests firmly at the door of the ruling Liberal Democrats. They legitimized racism and by consequence provided impetus and scope for the BNP's racial populism to spread. At one level, whilst the Liberal Democrats were attempting to hold on to political power by encouraging racial prejudice from above, 'below', at street-level, the BNP were sinking local roots into a territory made fertile by institutionalized racism and individual anomie. And it was this continuing process that in the end produced the cycle of BNP growth.

In due course the BNP's racial populism gained further ground by simply bringing the 'racist' stance of the Liberal Democrats into doubt. The simplistic yet potent charge the BNP levelled against the Liberal Democrats was that for all their 'racism', once in power, they betrayed whites and always favoured Bangladeshis. This was the line of attack that Osborne adopted in his election literature in 1992: 'The Liberals' Sons and Daughters scheme is just a con – Bangladeshis are still put first in housing in Liberal Neighbourhoods like Bethnal Green and Poplar' (*Island Patriot* BNP leaflet, 1992) and Beackon repeated this verbatim in September 1993 in his election literature (see *Spearhead*, No. 303, May 1994, p. 14). Undoubtedly the BNP's propaganda must have appeared persuasive, especially when housing allocations to larger properties such as Masthouse Terrace in the Isle of Dogs were made to Bangladeshis (who were particularly affected by homelessness and overcrowding). This particular allocation produced a storm of local controversy creating the impression that the finest public housing always went to ethnic minorities in the first instance.

Perhaps the BNP hit the nail on the head when, following Beackon's election victory, it commented: 'The Liberals repeated last year's shabby trick of playing the "race card", by trying to pretend that they were against immigration. The trick failed, as local whites had heard it all before, and this time were not taken in' (*British Nationalist*, October 1993, p. 1).

FUTURE PROSPECTS FOR THE BNP: A NATIONAL BREAKTHROUGH?

> Millwall was just the beginning. The British National Party will soon be enjoying greater electoral sucesses.
> (*British Nationalist*, October 1993, p. 1)

These raised expectations were seemingly thwarted when Derek Beackon lost his council seat in Millwall in May 1994. Reassuringly the BNP's electoral victory the year before now appeared to be a 'one-off' protest vote that had promptly evaporated. Yet this comforting impression is rather deceptive. Closer inspection of the local council elections in May 1994 reveals that, not only had Beackon polled an extra 561 votes, but throughout Tower Hamlets, the BNP's share of the vote had increased considerably. In the four wards of Tower Hamlets, the combined vote for the BNP was 28 per cent, 25 per cent, 22 per cent and 20 per cent (see *Spearhead*, No. 312, February 1995, p. 5). Ominously the BNP also captured a combined 33 per cent of the vote in one ward in the neighbouring borough of Newham where it contested seats for the first time. Newham is similarly an area of socio-economic deprivation and deindustrialization; it also contains a high ethnic minority population. In total the BNP presented 29 candidates, the majority of which contested seats in the London area. Here, the BNP garnered some 13,731 votes overall with a 'respectable' average of 8.39 per cent per candidate (see *Searchlight*, No. 228, June 1994, p. 4). These results hardly convey the look of a party in decline, and although the BNP's 'moment of destiny' had clearly not arrived at Millwall, these recent electoral gains do suggest that the BNP has become increasingly established in Tower Hamlets and that its support base is expanding into neighbouring areas. While accepting that this support remains relatively circumscribed in East London, the fact that the BNP is realizing its support potential around the race issue in these, albeit spatially confined areas does raise the possibility of wider growth. Nevertheless, as it will be argued, the spectre of a national breakthrough for contemporary fascism in Britain still remains improbable.

According to BNP's Campaigns Organizer Eddy Butler, localized campaigning is *the* path to follow if support for the BNP is to grow more widely: 'Success in one location breeds interest in us over a much wider area, and hence greater success' (*Spearhead*, No. 281, July 1992, p. 10). The local elections of May 1994 suggest that this growth strategy may contain some mileage. Arguably the BNP's victory in Tower Hamlets in 1993 produced a 'Millwall effect' where, as a consequence of the BNP demonstrating a tangible capacity to succeed in Millwall, voters in neighbouring areas felt that opting for the BNP in May 1994 would not necessarily entail a 'wasted vote'. But perhaps more important was the fact that, as in Tower Hamlets, the race issue was also politicized locally in Newham but this time by the Conservative Party where four candidates stood as 'Conservatives Against Labour's Unfair Ethnic Policies' and where previously a racist leaflet had been distributed by Newham South Conservatives at a by-election in 1993 (see *The Enemy In Our Midst*, 1995, pp. 17–21). This aspect seems to further confirm that the BNP's growth largely depends on mainstream politicization of race to create its political space. Where race remains depoliticized, the BNP's political space is necessarily compressed.

Yet even in the absence of mainstream race politicization, the BNP still believes that the process of localized concentration will eventually produce a sequence whereby its credibility, legitimacy and profile will progressively rise, culminating in a national breakthrough over the longer term: 'If we can replicate the East End situation in 20 other locations around the country, our national profile, and hence our attractiveness in all areas, will rise' (*Spearhead*, No. 281, July 1992, p. 9). Therefore, the future direction of the BNP will see, as Tyndall writes: '... a continuation of the increased emphasis on preparation for elections that has marked party development during the 1990s' (*Spearhead*, No. 311, January 1995, p. 5). However, the failure of the British National Party to retain its seat in Millwall has been a major psychological blow for the party resulting in a significant fall in morale at the grassroots (see *Spearhead*,

No. 312, February 1995, p. 5). BNP activists are being increasingly pulled away by the more 'stimulating' activities of the violent neo-Nazi 'Combat 18' group which means that this long-term growth strategy of the British National Party, which is dependent on tireless local activism, can only be impeded. Moreover, the assumption that the BNP will eventually prove attractive in all geographical areas fails to appreciate that, from the 1970s, greatest success for the far right in Britain (and for that matter France) has occurred in urban areas of high ethnic minority concentration, typically undergoing deindustrialization. In these 'anomic' areas where social life has been deregulated by uncompromising structural change, racism takes on importance as the only remaining source of viable 'community consciousness', but it remains an important consideration that these areas are geographically finite.

Perhaps it is instructive to compare the BNP's growth strategy with the experience of the Front National in France which developed a local 'fiefdom' at Dreux prior to its national breakthrough in 1984. Here Le Pen's former deputy Jean-Pierre Stirbois endeavoured to construct a localized support base from 1978. Already by 1979, the FN had made electoral gains at Dreux with Stirbois polling some 8.5 per cent of the vote in local elections. A pattern of growth was later confirmed when Stirbois polled 12.63 per cent of the vote in further local elections in March 1982. This concentration on Dreux was a key factor in the national electoral emergence of the FN because in September 1983, a rearranged municipal election at Dreux assumed national importance (at the time, Mitterrand's popularity rating was at the lowest level ever recorded for a President of the Fifth Republic). This gave the FN valuable national publicity and a subsequent electoral alliance with the moderate right during this election contest had the additional effect of awarding the Front National the prize of national political legitimacy. Decisively, the immediate reaction of the French media at both national and local levels to the FN (unlike the NF in the 1970s) was far from malevolent. Following Dreux and in the approach to the June 1984 European elections, important branches of the French media made Le Pen a figure of political importance in his own right and in the end, and to varying degrees, ultimately confirmed national political legitimacy on the Front National (see Charlot, 1986).

In contrast, the immediate media reaction to Beackon's

electoral victory in 1993 was overwhelming hostility. From the 'SIEG HEIL... and now he's a British councillor' front page headline of the *Daily Mirror* (18 September 1993, p. 1) to the more restrained 'RACE SHAME FOR LIBERALS' headline in the *Daily Mail* (18 September 1993, p. 1), the BNP was forced to acknowledge that: 'The official Media hate our guts' (*British Nationalist*, October 1993, p. 1). Even at the local level, although the *East London Advertiser* remained silent prior to the election, the *Docklands Recorder* (circulation: 28,000) called on its readers to resist voting BNP whose manifesto '... is based on hatred, no different in ideology to that of Mosley or Hitler' (15 September 1993, p. 1). This anti-BNP stance was repeated again in May 1994 (see *Docklands Recorder*, 4 May 1994, p. 6) when it was joined (at last) by the *East London Advertiser*, which urged its readers '... to take a few hours off, go and see *Schindlers List*, and see if you feel quite so content to vote for a party of the far right' (5 May 1994, p. 1). As was the case with the National Front in the 1970s (see Troyna, 1980; Troyna, 1982; Copsey, 1995) national and local press delegitimization does present a formidable barrier against wider growth for the BNP in the 1990s, especially when its own press has such a small circulation and it is so heavily dependent on the 'establishment' press for national publicity. Even if the BNP does manage to legitimate itself in a few concentrated areas through its local-issue campaigning, it seems unlikely that it could possibly move beyond this stage and achieve nationwide acceptability when the media is so antagonistic towards the BNP and it remains such a small party with such meagre resources.

In fact, national acceptancy seems even more of a remote possibility when the BNP (like the NF in the 1970s) persists with a revolutionary fascist agenda which is scarcely hidden (unlike the FN in France) and continues with a transparent, uncharismatic leadership (unlike Le Pen) which has a clear Nazi past (Tyndall was a prominent member of the National Socialist Movement in the early 1960s). Fortunately, the FN's style of 'careful nationalism' has never been the answer for the BNP. As the obdurate Tyndall wrote in 1988: 'Nothing creates such a pathetic spectacle as those people who live in daily dread of being branded "fascist" or "nazis" and are thus deterred from adopting any robust principles at all' (Tyndall, 1988, p. 592). Yet a by-product of such a careless approach is that Beackon, for instance, photographed giving a Nazi salute, can be freely paraded in the national newspapers (see *Daily Mirror*, 18 September 1993, p. 1).

Moreover, mainstream management of the race issue at the national level has generally served to contain the electoral appeal of the post-war extreme right in Britain (Eatwell, 1992) and there is little reason to suggest that this will not continue. In the immediate aftermath of the BNP's election victory in 1993, Home Secretary Michael Howard maintained that the key to amicable race relations was a 'firm immigration policy' (*The Guardian*, 18 September 1993, p. 26) which merely reiterated the established Conservative maxim that the way to prevent a rise in fascism is through 'tough' immigration policies. However, if in the near future the race issue is carelessly *mis*managed at the national level (in France, the rise of the FN came after a perceived laxity in French immigration policy) and is sensationally politicized in such a way that the racist constituency feels that white interests have been 'betrayed' by mainstream politicians (as in Tower Hamlets) then legitimate political space for the BNP at the national level may well open up. But without substantial internal moderation (as was the case with the FN after 1978) and a change of leadership it is implausible to suppose that the BNP could *consolidate* this space given the ill-considered manner in which it lays itself open to fascist 'smear' campaigns by both the media and anti-fascist groups.

A more obvious factor militating against a national breakthrough for the BNP is the British electoral system. According to Tyndall's conspiratorial perspective: 'The British system of "first-past-the-post" is tailor-made to protect that "inner" establishment that acts as the real power in British politics by way of controlling the three major parties, including, most importantly, the two which habitually win elections under the system as it is' (*British Nationalist*, May 1992, p. 4). Not surprisingly the BNP favours the introduction of proportional representation to confer minor parties with greater parliamentary representation so that voting for the extreme right at the national level is no longer a squandered vote. In France, PR in 1984 and 1986 undeniably assisted the rise of the FN, but in addition, the current two-ballot majority system in France also lends itself to 'legitimizing' electoral agreements of the type that occurred at Dreux in 1983. In Britain, the properties of the electoral system preclude electoral agreements of kindred stock.

Consequently the BNP finds itself distanced from the moderate right and remains largely unable to assemble political legitimacy through electoral cooperation. So, while the FN in the 1980s was integrated into moderate right space, in part as a result of local and regional electoral contracts, in Britain, this avenue for legitimation remains institutionally forbidding and is therefore effectively closed.

For these reasons, contemporary fascism in Britain is condemned to remain on the very fringes of mainstream national politics. Drawing this chapter to its close, it does seem highly unlikely that the BNP could possibly spring from spatially concentrated local success to national significance. The BNP has reached an impasse which without substantive future success threatens to seriously debilitate it. Tyndall's claim that: 'We have set in motion something that no power can possibly stop. We are part of a tide of history that is now irresistible' (*Spearhead*, No. 303, May 1994, p. 4) appears on reflection little more than a pipe dream, the sort of futile fancy that sanguine leaders of the British fascism find especially difficult to recant. More worrying than the possible threat of the BNP's national electoral emergence, however, is the deep-rooted racial intolerance which permeates mainstream British culture and which invites local electoral success for fascist organizations like the BNP to act as a catalyst for racial violence. (It was reported in *The Guardian*, 18 March 1994, p. 10, that the number of racial incidents in the East End following the election of Beackon had increased by 300 per cent.) With the number of racial attacks in Britain conservatively estimated to be in the region of 130–140,000 a year (see Kushner, 1994, p. 37) the more substantial problem is not necessarily contemporary fascism as such, but racism. It is in this context, where racism permeates mainstream British culture and provides the potential reservoir of support for fascism, that the real lesson of Tower Hamlets should be located. And this lesson is a simple one – irresponsible manipulation of the race issue is playing with fire.

ACKNOWLEDGEMENTS

I would like to thank Tony Robson and Louise Procter for providing materials and Richard Copsey for his comments on an early draft.

REFERENCES

Charlot, M., 'L'émergence du Front National', *Revue Française de Science Politique*, Vol. 36, No. 1, 1986, pp. 30–45.
Copsey, N., 'Fascism: the ideology of the BNP', *Politics*, Vol. 14, No. 3, 1994, pp. 101–8.
Copsey, N., 'The Extreme Right in Contemporary France and Britain', unpublished PhD thesis, 1995.
Eatwell, R., 'Why has the extreme right failed in Britain?' in Hainsworth, P. (ed.), *The Extreme Right in Europe and the USA* (London, 1992), pp. 175–92.
Fekete, L., 'UK commentary: Europe for the Europeans: East End for the East Enders', *Race and Class*, Vol. 32, No. 1, 1990, pp. 66–76.
Griffin, R., *The Nature of Fascism* (London, 1991).
Harris, G., *The Dark Side of Europe. The Extreme Right Today* (Edinburgh, 1990).
Hill, R. with Bell, A., *The Other Face of Terror* (London, 1988).
Kushner, T., 'The fascist as "other"? Racism and neo-Nazism in contemporary Britain', *Patterns of Prejudice*, Vol. 28, No. 1, 1994, pp. 27–45.
Lowndes, V. and Stoker, G., 'An evaluation of neighbourhood decentralisation', *Policy and Politics*, Vol. 20, No. 1, 1992, pp. 47–61.
Messina, A., *Race and Party Competition in Britain* (Oxford, 1989).
Payne, S., *Fascism* (Madison, 1980).
Thurlow, R., *Fascism in Britain* (Oxford, 1987).
Troyna, B., 'The media and the electoral decline of the National Front', *Patterns of Prejudice*, Vol. 14, No. 3, 1980, pp. 25–30.
Troyna, B., 'Reporting the National Front: British values observed', in Husband, C. (ed.), *Race in Britain. Continuity and Change* (London, 1982), pp. 259–78.
Tyndall, J., *The Eleventh Hour* (London, 1988).

Newspapers, journals and reports

At War With Society (*Searchlight*, July 1993).
British Eastender.
British Nationalist.
CARF.
Constitution of the British National Party.
Liberal Democrat Report: *Political Speech and Race Relations in a Liberal Democracy*, Report of an Inquiry into the conduct of the Tower Hamlets Liberal Democrats in publishing allegedly racist election literature between 1990 and 1993 (December 1993).
Searchlight.
Spearhead.
The Enemy in Our Midst (Newham Monitoring Project, 1995).

8 British Fascism: The Ugly Duckling
Roger Griffin

THE NEED TO PLACE BRITISH FASCISM WITHIN A WIDER CONTEXT

By concentrating on the reasons for the failure of specific forms of British fascism primarily from a historiographical and Anglocentric point of view, it is easy to lose sight of structural causes at work which arguably help determine the fate of *any* specimen of the fascist genus. At the risk of disconcerting or alienating readers concerned with the unique events and facts which make up history in the sense of 'how it actually was', this essay will concentrate on sketching out a model designed to throw into relief the factors which condition its viability as a genus of modern political ideology. The aim is bring out the fact that the failure of the individual fascisms which have been the subject of earlier chapters was in no way exceptional, but part of a pattern exhibited by nearly all their blood relatives in other countries.

In this 'nomothetic' perspective the surface texture of history, which under an 'ideographic' lens is revealed in such microscopic detail, becomes a shadowy blur, and it is the skeleton and vital organs underneath which come into focus. In the case of fascism, a more gruesome biological metaphor suggests itself. What comparative studies produce is ecographs of countless embryonic fascist movements contained within the body politic of modern nation-states which mercifully never progress beyond a rudimentary stage in their development, and just a few which grow further only to die long before emerging as a fully-fledged political regime. Seen generically, fascism is thus an abortive political movement in the overwhelming majority of cases, and British fascism only confirms the rule.

It should be stressed at the outset that in focusing on the structural dimension so as to locate the fate of British fascist movements within their generic context, what follows sets out to complement the foregoing chapters, and not to imply the primacy of model building over empirical analysis. Nor is the spirit in which it is written determinist, but 'probabilistic'. It assumes that all historical events are realizations of potential realities contained in a particular configuration of economic, political, social, cultural and ideological structures. These structures make particular events more or less probable as actualizations of some of these potential realities, but their complexity precludes accurate predictions of what will happen at any given point, even if it allows a high degree of retrodiction.

It is this feature of human history that explains why historiography can operate very much as a social science in providing causal analyses of events, as long as it avoids monocausality and reductionism – in this sense the natural scientific discipline closest to historiography is perhaps meteorology. The variables involved in causing historical events, however, are in themselves so complex, and their interaction so resistant to accurate modelling, that even extremely short-term predictions are highly hazardous. Nevertheless, to identify the structural constraints which affect the way generic phenomena materialize in specific situations allows certain eventualities and outcomes relating to them to be ruled out a priori as highly unlikely.

In the case of fascism, this chapter will argue that it is intrinsic to its very nature as a political ideology that it will only come into being in the society of a particular kind of nation-state; that it will only develop into a significant popular movement when an unusual conjuncture of structural forces are present in that society; and that it will only be in a position to seize state power in a set of conditions so rare as to be considered 'freak'. The conclusion will be that Britain provides a case study of fascism in its 'normal', highly marginalized state, full of revolutionary aspirations and rhetoric which it is powerless to turn into reality.

THE DEFINITION OF FASCISM USED HERE

Clearly this argument assumes an operational definition of fascism, one of the most debated words in the political lexicon. The ideal type used here has been elaborated in *The Nature of*

Fascism (Griffin, 1991, 1993), and corroboration of its heuristic value in identifying a common ideological core to fascism has been provided by the scores of primary source extracts reproduced in *Fascism* (Griffin, 1995) published in the Oxford Readers series. Central to this ideal type is a concentration on the fascist's obsession with the nation's current decadence and imminent rebirth (palingenesis) in a nebulously conceived post-liberal new order. It is arguably this myth of the regenerated national community thriving with a new type of state which forms the elusive 'fascist minimum'. In other words it is the common denominator not only between the many different ideologies of national renewal which converged in fascism, but the programmes of the revolutionary nationalist movements most often associated with generic fascism (e.g. the Spanish Falange, the Romanian Iron Guard, the Finnish IKL), despite significant surface divergences conditioned by the unique historical situation and cultural climate of each nation-state concerned. This ideal type of generic fascism can be formulated as follows: *Fascism is a genus of political ideology whose mythic core in its various permutations is a palingenetic form of populist ultra-nationalism.* Subsumed within this one-sentence definition are a number of the features frequently included in the 'list-definitions' to which many commentators have had recourse when characterizing generic fascism (see Griffin, 1995, pp. 1–10).

As examples of how this ideal type applies to two specimens of British fascism, what stands out in the ideology of the BUF is the radical critique of the country's existing parliamentary and economic system, the weakness and ineptitude of her governing class (the 'old gang'), and her decline both as an imperial world power and as a manufacturing and trading nation, all set against the spiritual and cultural anarchy which is affecting 'modern' society, and the pervasive crisis of liberalism, free-market capitalism, Europe and Western civilization in general. This picture of decadence is no cultural pessimism, however, for it forms one panel of a diptych, the other of which portrays Britain in the imminent future under a new strong state led by an inspired leader, with a revitalized industry based on a new technocratic elite working within a corporative economy on the behalf of a national community of 'true' Britons. Such a community would be secure from the threat of communism and internal strife, imbued once more with a new heroic spirit of patriotism, community and historical purpose. In other words the BUF worked for Britain's rebirth, or what Mosley called 'a Greater Britain'. It is this myth that forms the subtext of all its literature, rallies, and speeches, occasionally manifesting itself textually as well, as in the following BUF marching song:

Britain Awake!

Britain awake! Arise from slumber!
Soon comes the daybreak of Rebirth.
We lift again thy trampled banners,
Our marching legions shake the earth.
We gather from thy lanes and cities,
With men of action at our head.
In us division and delusion,
And all hypocrisies are dead.
We follow Fascism and Mosley,
We fight for freedom and for bread!

We bring a saving Revolution,
We are aweary of deceit.
We will avenge the long betrayal,
We will acknowledge no defeat.
We breathe the spirit of our fathers,
As dauntless and as proud as they.
O'erthrow the tyranny of falsehood –
The powers of darkness and decay!
We will be victors of tomorrow,
Who are the victims of today!

Britain, assert thine ancient honour,
Who never knew a foreign yoke.
Oh, turn thy face toward the future;
Thy life and strength are in thy folk.
If Britain to herself be faithful,
And each man to his fellow true,
Through all the world come forth against us,
We even yet shall make them rue.
We'll build a Britain fit for heroes,
With courage fresh and splendour new.

(R.R. Bellamy, 'Official History of the BUF' (unpublished), 1939, pp. 95–6; quoted Griffin, 1995, 173–80)

The pervasive presence of the same mythic matrix can be documented in post-war British fascism. One exhaustive exposition of its characteristic ideology has been supplied in recent years by John Tyndall, one-time leader of Britain's National Front and now of the British National Party in his book *The Eleventh Hour: A Call for British Rebirth*. After a vitriolic attack on the state of contemporary Britain, which he presents as infected by 'spiritual AIDS', the final chapter concludes with this florid passage:

> From out of the chaos and the ruins wrought by the old politics, new men are rising. These new men of the new age are now working night and day across the land to forge the sinews of the movement to which their lives and mine are dedicated. Above them as they work are the spirits of legions of mighty ancestors whose bones lie at the bottom of the oceans and beneath the soil of five continents where the men and women of our blood have borne the British flag and stamped the mark of British genius. Today we feel the voices of these past generations calling down to us in sacred union, urging us to be worthy of their example and their sacrifice. To them we owe it to fight on, and to dare all, so that a great land and a great race may live again in splendour.
> (Tyndall, 1988; quoted Griffin, 1995, 368–70)

THE STRUCTURAL PRECONDITIONS FOR FASCISM TO 'SUCCEED'

One implication of the centrality to fascism of the archetypal myth of phoenix-like rebirth combined with populist ultranationalism is that as an ideological force it can only emerge in a specific type of society at a particular point in its development. Its preconditions are (a) an established nation-state (which precludes separatist nationalist movements, as well as totally artificial new nation-states not based on a strong ethnically or historically based sense of national identity); in which (b) 'modernization' has eroded traditional power to a point where a plurality of secular ideologies (and, possibly, politicized religions) vie for hegemony; where (c) populist nationalism is a potent (if dormant) force; where (d) the concept of cultural decadence and national weakness can be transformed into a sense of national regeneration; and where (e) history has provided the basis for a myth of former greatness of the 'people' (even if not formally constituted as a nation-state) which can thus rationalize a sense of decline or decay and the prospect of a rebirth inspired by the past, but not a literal reversion to it. Given these preconditions, it is no coincidence if palingenetic forms of ultra-nationalism, which can now be seen as anticipating the fully fledged fascism that emerged after 1918, first appeared in France, Italy and Germany (see Griffin, 1993, 200–5).

Once fascism exists in theory as an ideology, or in practice as an organization, it encounters major obstacles to doing more than vegetating as a minuscule and often fissiparous movement marginalized by existing cultural and political forces. What prevents it from bursting into full bloom as a revolutionary threat to the status quo can be reduced to three major factors. Firstly, the problem of being a late-comer into a society in which a welter of non- and tendentially anti-fascist political and cultural forces already exist, thus creating a lack of 'political space'. Secondly, the internal problems of creating a cohesive movement faced by any new political formation. Thirdly, the problem of being a revolutionary political creed, and hence a force which except in the most exceptional historical conditions will only appeal 'naturally' to a small minority of temperaments – most people being by nature reactionary/conservative or reformist/gradualistic in their politics, if not apolitical. This radically narrows the potential support base for fascism's intensely revolutionary and utopian form of politics (see Griffin, 1993, ch. 8).

To have sufficient political space to flourish, a fascist movement must operate in a society in which the hegemony of the traditional, conservative right has been severely weakened by the inroads of liberal-capitalist modernity. In other words, the power of secularization, urbanization, literacy, social mobility, pluralism, party politics, free-market economy, consumerism, mass communications, etc., must have combined to undermine the social and ideological foundations on which the traditional power system hitherto depended, allowing for a degree of populist nationalism and of the 'massification' of society to take place. In that sense fascism is very much a 'modern ideology', for it can only emerge at all in at least partially modernized nation-states. Where traditional societies still hold sway, as in large parts of Africa, the Middle East and Asia in the inter-war period, fascism cannot take root. Where the traditional right is still strong in modern guise, as in Latin America and Japan, fascism will inevitably be crushed if it ever threatens the hegemony of the established power elite.

At the same time, where the ultra-left has achieved hegemony through revolution, as it did in Russia after 1917, this also effectively closes off any viable space in which alternative revolutionary ideologies such as fascism can operate. On the other hand, where liberalism, a concomitant of modernity but not to be equated with it, has established itself to a point where a pluralistic society and a political system based on what Norberto Bobbio calls democracy's 'rules of the game' enjoys general, if tacit, acceptance, then the space for fascism will also be highly restricted.

It is in connection with the latter point that 'crisis' comes to play a vital role in enlarging the space available for a fascist assault on society. An outstanding example of such a crisis was the one which emerged in a number of countries in the aftermath of the First World War, especially when it unleashed a wave of socio-economic instability compounded by a (largely perceived) threat from the ultra-left. In some states this was able to destabilize the liberal political system, thus undermining its perceived legitimacy. Wherever this occurred in a state in which the traditional monarchical, religious or military right was too weak to rally, take the initiative and (re-)assert its authority, the fascist claim to represent the only force which could put an end to the crisis and regenerate the nation in a new order based on populism rather than traditional hierarchy proved able to exert a wide enough appeal to elements within a range of different social groups to become an incipient mass movement.

However, a crucial factor which influenced events in the inter-war period was the subjective sense of crisis. If the sense of nationhood was in the main highly stable, if nationalistic aspirations were generally sated, if the legitimacy of existing constitutional arrangements was widely taken for granted, if liberal taboos against violence or radical change were well entrenched, then even a profound socio-economic and political crisis would tend to be resolved without whipping up extra-systemic or extra-parliamentary forces. In other words, without a generalized 'sense-making crisis' (Platt, 1980) which called the status quo and all prevailing norms into question, fascism was impotent. But where objective pressures on the legitimacy of the existing liberal order created a resonance with widely held misgivings about its legitimacy and its capacity to deal with the crisis, it cast deep subjective doubts on whether the constitutional arrangements in which it is embodied were not in fact alien to the national tradition, or an obstacle to its regeneration. At this point a fascist organization could find itself with increased room to manoeuvre, and become a fully fledged 'mass movement'. This happened in Italy between 1920 and 1922, Germany between 1930 and 1933, Finland between 1932 and 1936, and Brazil between 1934 and 1937 (see Griffin, 1993, chs 2, 3, 5, 6). It was able to do so because those convinced of the need for drastic action to solve the perceived national crisis (and thus predisposed both to revolution and ultra-nationalism) were lured by fascism's palingenetic remedies to 'save' the nation and create a healthy national community.

To take advantage of the external situation described the movement itself must have a number of intrinsic qualities. It must have a degree of organizational coherence and dynamism, and a national leadership strong enough to provide a sense of direction and purpose, but not so autocratic as to stifle the initiative and zeal of leaders lower down the hierarchy. Its sense of being a dynamic movement must be fed not only by effective programmes, rhetoric and propaganda, but rallies and ritualistic events orchestrated to generate a sense of community and strength. These will serve to complement those spheres of action where militant members can feel they are part of a revolutionary vanguard.

Tactically, too, the national and local leadership must be sufficiently alert to respond to any issues generated by the flow of events on which an ideological stand or decisive action can be taken. In practice a fascist movement will be at its most effective operating both legally at the level of pressure group or political party and illegally by recourse to the rhetorical or actual violence typical of a paramilitary formation. In its jockeying for position to present itself as a credible basis of a new political order it will be important for a fascist movement to attract the tacit support or collusion of conservative forces. In other words it must be prepared to woo non-revolutionary elements within the monarchy, army, civil service, big business and social elites who share fascist concerns about the threats to the institutions of the nation posed by its alleged internal and external enemies. If it succeeds in capitalizing on conservative scepticism about the capacity of liberal democracy to resolve the deep-seated causes of the nation's decadence, and in turning it into passive acceptance of or active collusion with their cause, then fascists will have gained invaluable allies for the carrying out of their revolution.

The last point also has a bearing on the paradox that the very strength that fascism's palingenetic, and hence revolutionary, goals gives it in mobilizing its most ardent supporters also constitutes a major source of weakness. As we have already pointed out, in a pluralistic modern society it is a minority which is naturally endowed with a revolutionary temperament, one which looks beyond the status quo with its existing institutions and ideologies to an unprecedented new order based on political change brought about by human agency. For fascism to have as wide an appeal as possible it is essential that its central myth of the regenerated national community acts as a sort of ideological Rorschach test, one which allows revolutionaries of various hues, some even former socialist radicals, to read into it their own diagnosis of the 'decadence' of the present society and their own remedy for its ills. The nebulousness of fascism's ideal of what is to replace the present is essential to achieving this effect, as is the incorporation of elements which can appeal to various social groups, the young, militarists, workers, the middle class, farmers, big business, nationalists, women, intellectuals, the left as well as the right.

A concomitant of this nebulousness is the significant part played, in those fascist movements which succeed in attracting a mass following, by a style of politics which is populist rather than elitist, and charismatic rather than rational. In other words, to be successful a fascist movement or regime must generate a sense of political liturgy and civic religion. The leader cult is an obvious symptom of this tendency, but by no means the only one. It is an integral part of inter-war fascism's disparagement of doctrines and programmes, of its celebration of a total 'world view', of its stress on the 'movement' aspect of the fascist struggle for power rather than its 'merely' party aspect. Equally important are fascism's tendency to make the movement's symbol as ubiquitous as possible, the preference for highly emotive 'rallies' (often held at night) rather than meetings which would allow for genuine discussion, and the celebration of the mythic over the intellectual – which in practice often came down to an insistence on simple slogans rather than theoretical analysis as the key to disseminating fascism's 'truth'. Hitler himself was all too aware of this aspect of fascism when he wrote:

> The receptive powers of the masses are very restricted, and their understanding feeble. On the other hand, they quickly forget. Such being the case, all effective propaganda must be confined to a few bare essentials and those must be expressed as far as possible in stereotyped formulas. These slogans should be persistently repeated until the very last individual has come to grasp the idea that has been put forward.
> (Hitler, 1939, 159)

Such insights into the art of persuasion should not detract attention away from the fact that fascist ideology is not to be reduced to propaganda. Fascist social engineering has the goal of creating not a robot, but a new man, and the words from Hitler just quoted are to be set against the far more revealing declaration attributed to him by Rauschning:

> We had come to a turning-point in world history – that was his constant theme ... He saw himself as chosen for superhuman tasks, as the prophet of the rebirth of man in a new form. Humanity, he proclaimed, was in the throes of a vast metamorphosis ... The coming age was revealing itself in the first great human figures of a new type ... 'Those who see in National Socialism nothing more than a political movement know scarcely anything of it. It is even more than a religion: it is the will to create mankind anew.'
> (Rauschning, 1939, 240–2)

THE INTER-WAR PERIOD AND THE FREAK SUCCESS OF FASCISM AND NAZISM

In the light of the above it should now be clear why the 'classic' era of fascism occurred in the inter-war period. The First World War created a welter of social, economic, political and psychological upheavals and dysfunctions configured differently in all the nations of Europe, thus producing a wide range of different outcomes. In Russia it led to a revolution, which by convincing many revolutionary 'Bolsheviks' throughout the world that the new age of proletarian hegemony prophesied by Marx was nigh, and even persuading many visceral anti-Marxists that Bolshevism posed a serious threat to society, added a new dimension of destabilization and trauma. Yet though the 'red peril' created anxieties for liberals, conservatives and populist nationalists throughout the Western world, the preconditions for fascism's take-off outlined above materialized only in a small number of countries. In countries where liberalism was weak and the power of the traditional right still strong, fascism was either marginalized and partially co-opted (as in Schuschnigg's Austria or Franco's Spain), or marginalized and suppressed (as in Salazar's Portugal or Horthy's Hungary, Chile, Brazil, Japan, Bulgaria and the Baltic States). In Romania both strategies were used: the embodiment of the monarchical right, King Carol, attempted first to suppress the Iron Guard, then to co-opt it, while his successor, General Antonescu, first tried to co-opt it, only to resort subsequently to crushing it with Hitler's connivance. Meanwhile, in liberal countries where the traditional ultra-right was weak or non-existent, as in Iceland, Denmark, Holland, Norway and Switzerland, fascism was simply marginalized, at least till the Second World War. Belgium, Czechoslovakia and Poland hosted various types of religious, secular, ethnic and nationalist ultra-right and ultra-nationalism, but had little in the way of genuine fascism in the 1930s.

It was only in a small group of countries where democratic institutions had established themselves in historically old nations but had not yet put down deep roots, where the traditional ultra-right was too debilitated by modernization to seize power, and where a particularly strong conjuncture of destabilizing forces existed, that fascism had a look-in at all. These were Finland, Italy and Germany. In Finland, despite propitious conditions created by the war of liberation from Russia and the emergence of a powerful fascist force out of what had been a primarily anti-communist movement, liberal democratic institutions just held out. In Italy and Germany too, conjunctural forces meant that fascism became powerful movements. Yet it was contingent events (associated with *squadrismo*, the March on Rome and the Matteotti assassination in Italy; the world-wide Depression, the phase of presidential governments, the miscalculations of and the fortuitous election and untimely death of Hindenburg in Germany) which actually created opportunities for them to enter the citadel of the state.

Once there they were true to their nature, consolidating their grip on power, eradicating effective opposition, and thus placing themselves in a position to attempt to actualize their schemes for the 'total' New Order. However, the success of Mussolini and Hitler in making their fascism exceptions to the rule of its marginalization under democratic regimes is to be attributed also to the inability of liberal institutions and conservative establishments debilitated by a complex of historical and structural factors to shut them out from power, rather than to the intrinsic power of fascism itself. Fascism is by no means as irresistible as its own propaganda implies, which explains the subtitle to Brecht's satire of Hitler's career, the *stoppable* rise of Arturo Ui. A nexus of miscalculations and ineptitude combined with a disastrous misreading of the implications of fascist radicalism, and of the threat it posed to liberal and conservative values alike, compliantly opened the gates to the Trojan horse of palingenetic ultra-nationalism (see Griffin, 1993, ch. 8).

THE FAILURE OF THE BUF AS A SYMPTOM OF MORE GENERAL PATTERN

The inability of fascism to threaten the stability of British society in the inter-war period is thus hardly to be seen as an exceptional phenomenon, but rather the exemplification of a general syndrome of impotence and marginalization. The formations of the 1920s, such as the British Fascisti, made a minuscule impact on the country's political system, which stayed staunchly democratic. The resilience of British democracy to the threats (condemned to remain overwhelmingly rhetorical) of both the ultra-right and ultra-left is to be explained by the conjuncture of a number of factors, notably: (a) Britain had a long-standing tradition of gradualism and constitutionalism; (b) it had been a victor in the First World War; (c) it had thus retained its constitutional monarchy, parliamentary system and empire not just intact but consolidated: its nationalism was 'sated'; (d) victory in 1918 had confirmed most Britons' assumption that their land was an unassailable Great Power; (e) Bolshevism was a minute political constituency. In the broad sense Britain is comparable to the USA, Canada, non-Finnish Scandinavia, Iceland, Switzerland, Holland, the Irish Republic and Belgium (though the domestic political situation of each and the fate of the extremist politics they hosted in each case is of course unique). Even in nominally democratic countries where dysfunctional factors and illiberal forces were much stronger, such as France, Czechoslovakia, Romania, Poland, Portugal, Greece and Austria, fascism never seriously threatened to carry out a revolution (though in all but the first two democracy had succumbed to conservative authoritarianism by 1939: see Griffin, 1993, pp. 213–17).

In the 1930s new factors crowded in thick and fast to create a cumulative sense of world crisis and liberal impotence: the effects of the Depression, the establishment of a stable authoritarian regime in Fascist Italy, the rise of Nazism and its eventual seizure of power, the perceived deterioration of the international situation underlined by the weakness of the League of Nations in dealing with Germany's reversal of the Versailles Treaty, Italy's conquest of Ethiopia, Japanese imperial expansion and the Spanish Civil War. It was against the background of a world crisis of liberalism and capitalism, one which was far from simply subjective, that a number of ultra-right movements and regimes emerged more or less modelled on Fascism and Nazism, at least as far as external trappings were concerned, and sometimes direct emulations of them: examples are the Blueshirts in Ireland, Rexism in Belgium, the Falange in Spain, the Scythe Cross and Arrow Cross in Hungary. Yet, this second tide of fascist activity too singularly failed to breach the defences of the state. Where conservative forces modernized themselves with sufficient energy they simply nipped fascism in the bud: this was the fate which befell Rolão Preto's National Syndicalists in Salazar's 'New State', for example. In Austria too the 'parafascist' Christian and corporatist state held out under Schuschnigg despite the assassination of his predecessor Dollfuss by (Austrian) Nazis, at least until the *Anschluss* with Germany was forced through by Hitler. This pattern was followed outside Europe wherever fascism came up against a previously established authoritarian regime, as in Chile, Brazil and Japan. The closest fascism got to conquering state power before 1939 was in Spain and Romania, where at least for a time military and monarchical forces were prepared to co-opt fascism in order to impart to their regime a pseudo-populist and pseudo-revolutionary dimension which neutralized significant areas of potential resistance.

Where liberal democracy held sway (albeit with various degrees of concession to authoritarianism or the strong state in the cause of the 'national interest' and 'national solidarity'), fascism was denied even this temporary concession. In one way or another it remained marginalized and impotent. The peaking of BUF membership at around 50,000 in 1934, its failure to trouble the stability of the British government, its eventual decline in membership and the internment of many of its followers during the war is just one permutation of a systematic pattern of failure exhibited in Switzerland, Holland, Belgium, Scandinavia, the Irish Republic, as well as the British Dominions (notably South Africa) and the United States. It was in Finland, a newly independent nation with enormous structural and geopolitical forces undermining its democratic institutions, that home-grown fascism came closest to breaking through, but nevertheless the state's liberal institutions proved resilient. Four other countries in which liberal institutions were sorely tested in the 1930s, certainly more so than Britain's, were Belgium, Norway, Holland and France. But in each case the state just managed to weather the anti-democratic storm: it was only Nazi occupation which gave indigenous fascism some nominal power once its leaders had adopted a 'collaborationist' stance by convincing themselves and their most faithful followers that their countries were about to become partners of the Third Reich in the New European Order. There is every likelihood that some prominent members of the BUF would have followed the examples of Degrelle, Quisling, Mussert and Doriot, possibly even Mosley himself, had Britain been occupied by the Nazis. The fate of the Ossewabrandwag, which also showed itself prepared to collude with Nazism in order to gain power, but comprehensively failed in turning South Africa into an Axis power, further confirms the pattern.

What is highlighted by this whirlwind tour of inter-war fascism is thus not so much the fragility of liberal democracy in the inter-war period, but its resilience (at least till Hitler launched Nazism into its imperialist phase). Where it was planted in shallow, contaminated or virgin soil, as in Spain, Portugal, Hungary, Poland, Austria and Yugoslavia, it could not long withstand the double wave of tremors stemming from the First World War and the Russian Revolution, and relapsed into authoritarianism. Wherever it had been able to put down a healthy taproot well *before* 1914, however, it proved remarkably hardy. Even Romania, where liberal-democracy had the most fragile hold on political life, held out against authoritarianism till the eve of the Second World War. Just as mercury is a freak metal in that in normal atmospheric conditions it is encountered in a liquid rather than solid state, so Fascism and Nazism are freak examples of generic fascism. They alone were able to harden into the solid state of a regime, rather than remain confined to fascism's much more familiar states of liquid (i.e. movement) and air (i.e. ideology), and even their ideological purity was severely compromised by extensive collusion with conservative forces. Once placed in an international context, Mosley's party can be seen to have done remarkably well to gain as many as 50,000 supporters and retain a high public profile for as long as it did. As a revolutionary threat to the system it so despised, though, it remained far less substantial than the 'Bolshevik' threat had been after 1918 in countries such as Hungary, Germany, Austria and Italy, where fears and perceptions also grossly exaggerated the real dangers it posed.

Naturally, historians are perfectly justified in identifying the specific factors which account for the BUF's comprehensive failure to seize power in Britain. Robert Benewick, for example, stresses as the 'immediate causes of its success and failure' (a) the absence of a concerted Marxist threat to the status quo; (b) the alienating impact of the BUF's espousal of anti-Semitism and of its use of violence; weaknesses in the leadership qualities of Oswald Mosley; (c) internal tensions within the BUF movement itself; (d) the effect of the creation of the 'National Government' in creating the impression that a trans-party alliance had been forged to deal with Britain's socioeconomic crisis; and (e) the fact that the crisis itself never reached the proportions that Mosley anticipated so that the preconditions for the credibility of the extra-systemic solution which his movement proposed never materialized. However, when he stresses the fact that BUF policy was only one of 'various descriptions and prescriptions for Britain's difficulties' and that the broad consensus on the desirability and viability of liberal democracy meant that 'Fascism as an alternative to parliamentary democracy failed to stimulate the imagination of the British public', he is not referring to qualities peculiar to Britain, but to the power of pluralism and the values of civil society comprehensively to thwart fascist assaults on state power in *all* liberal democracies, with the conspicuous exception of Italy and Germany (Benewick, 1971, pp. 300–4). Similarly, when Kenneth Lunn and Richard Thurlow stated that 'the failure of British fascist movements in the political sphere can be explained both in terms of the reaction of the state and their own internal weaknesses' (Lunn and Thurlow, 1980, p. 10), such an assertion is incomplete as it stands. It is to be supplemented with the third factor with which this chapter is concerned: the structural forces which make fascism a born loser in modern societies, whether hegemony belongs to conservatism, liberalism or communism.

THE POST-WAR PERIOD AND THE PERSISTENT MARGINALIZATION OF FASCISM

Fascism had only managed to break through in two structurally flawed and debilitated liberal democracies in the inter-war period. This was despite the extraordinary conjuncture of forces generating a diffuse sense of national crisis and of the decadence of the West in those two decades throughout the developed world. After 1945 the odds were even more overwhelmingly stacked against a fascist success. Liberal democracy and capitalism rapidly re-established themselves west of the Iron Curtain, while east of it state communism smothered the germination of any ultra-nationalist initiatives (except those sponsored by the state itself). The pervasive sense of democratic renewal and material progress in the non-communist West eventually ensured that even the remaining pockets of authoritarianism in Spain and Portugal became unsustainable once Salazar and Franco had died, while attempts to establish it in Greece could not hold out for long (conditions in parts of Latin America were much more propitious for rabidly anti-communist military regimes or highly corrupt liberal ones right up to the 1980s). Even the vanquished Axis powers, Germany, Japan and eventually Italy, instead of being subjected to the conditions of national humiliation and socioeconomic dysfunction which undermined Weimar, entered a phase of unprecedented prosperity and stable democracy. (The current crisis of the Italian state should be taken as a sign of its belated maturation rather than its imminent demise.)

Not only were the structural preconditions for the propagation of virulent myths of imminent national palingenesis missing after 1945, but the outcome of the war itself ensured that the ultra-nationalist discourse in which such myths were couched, especially the utopian sense of national renewal and regeneration within a charismatically led new order, had now acquired for the bulk of the world's population grotesque connotations of fanaticism, war, starvation, terror, military and civilian deaths on an unimaginable scale and attempted genocide. The radical differences in the climate in which post-war fascisms have to operate in contrast with their inter-war forbears have recently been the subject of a major article by Diethelm Prowe (1994; see also Griffin, 1993, pp. 219–21).

This is not to say that fascism died in 1945. There has been no shortage of fascist ideologues or activists. Fascist groups and movements have continued to proliferate (see Ó Maoláin, 1987). Fascism has developed new discourses and exploited new issues (see Griffin, 1995, Part V). In Italy, for example, it has established a thriving publishing industry, was for a time a terrorist force to be reckoned with, and in the MSI gave rise to the most tenacious electoral fascist party in the world. Its offshoot, Gianfranco Fini's Alleanza Nazionale, a major player in post-Tangentopoli politics, advocates a platform of policies in which fascism has been so thoroughly sanitized and modernized as to lose all but a hint revolutionary radicalism, even if those steeped in the history of Italy since 1919 will have no trouble discerning a fascist subtext.

Predictably, those with more uncompromising palingenetic temperaments regard this 'post-fascism' as a sell-out, just as hardliners on the left see the British Labour Party without the Clause 4 commitment to the extensive nationalization of capitalist institutions as no longer socialist. But such misgivings on the part of hardliners have little practical relevance. The prospects of 'fascist democracy' being any more successful in overthrowing liberal capitalism than 'social democracy' has been to date are negligible. Even if Fini were to become Italy's prime minister and the Dr Jekyll of moderation revealed himself to be a fanatical Mr Hyde, the geopolitical and global economic nexus in which Italy finds itself enmeshed precludes the dismantling of the country's democratic institutions more effectively than any CIA countermeasures (not that the CIA has been overzealous in toppling right-wing authoritarian regimes in the past.)

In other countries fascism has not gone to such lengths to undergo a cosmetic 'make-over'. In the United States neo-Nazism has revivified the home-grown 'Christian' white supremacism of the Ku-Klux-Klan, and is an integral part of a virulent racist and anti-communist subculture which, though generally marginalized, can sometimes surface in official politics as the election of David Duke to the Louisiana House of Representatives in 1988 demonstrated. In the newly unified Germany neo-Nazism and crypto-fascist parties have profited from the conditions of socio-economic and ideological upheaval, especially in the former DDR, and been especially successful in having the rights to asylum made far more restrictive while leaving the ethnic principles enshrined in German citizenship laws intact. The former East bloc, especially Romania, Hungary and Russia, have since 1989 produced ideal conditions of objective socio-economic and political traumas with a diffused 'nomic crisis' in which recycled or new forms of fascism can be incubated. The success of Zhirinovsky's Liberal Democrats in gaining significant electoral support in December 1993 despite the overtly fascistic nature of many of its claims and policies should shatter the complacency of those who assumed that Soviet authoritarianism would somehow give way seamlessly to the wonders of Scandinavian liberal democracy rather than the horrors of Third World capitalism.

Yet even when these trouble spots are taken into account,

the prospect of an imminent fascist seizure of power at a national level anywhere in the liberal-capitalist world is as remote and fantastic as ever. The predictions of some pundits in the early 1990s – as in the issue of *Searchlight* No. 198 for December 1991 or Michael Schmidt's *The New Reich* (1993) (see also Prowe, 1994, p. 289) – that a Fourth Reich might conceivably be installed in the new Germany have proved an overreaction, especially given the extraordinary fragmentation of the German extreme right, the lack of any credible threat from the ultra-left, the consistently weak electoral support of radical right parties in relation to mainstream ones, and the impressive number of 'ordinary' German citizens who took part in anti-fascist demonstrations. In any case, the 30,000 estimated to be actively fascist in the Federal Republic in 1989 (Ford, 1992, p. 19) belonged to scores of different formations, and pale into insignificance in comparison to the 300,000 Germans who on the eve of the NSDAP's seizure of power in 1933 were members of the SA, and hence were the activists of a single movement. Moreover it was a movement which had already established a nationwide 'shadow-state' poised to take over power under a charismatic leader. In reality the taste in the former East Germany for such items of 'Western' decadence as consumer-durables and pornography can be said far to outweigh the taste for the asceticism and commitment often involved in extremist politics. Meanwhile anti-fascist activism (Antifa), Green alarm at the relentless destruction of the ecosystem under present human management, not to mention the overtly anti-nationalist and anti-fascist celebration of dance at the heart of the rave subculture, are far more significant symptoms of the mentality of the young in the new Germany than neo-Nazism. Even in Russia, where parallels with the crisis conditions of Weimar Germany are more persuasive, public hostility to Yeltsin's attempt to impose his authority over Chechnya by force suggests that when rhetoric turns to action as a basis for Russian foreign policy based on palingenetic ultra-nationalism along the lines suggested by Zhirinovsky, support for that policy is weak.

The stubborn fact is that to implement its utopian scheme of national rebirth fascism must seize power and form a regime, unless, that is, it has taken on board the 'right-wing Gramscianism' elaborated by the New Right since the late 1960s under the aegis of Alain de Benoist. This purely 'intellectual' movement has retained the palingenetic mindset characteristic of fascism, but has abandoned the paramilitary or electoral scenario for seizing power in favour of an assault on the 'cultural hegemony' of liberalism and this has been replaced by an overtly anti-egalitarian ethos as the precondition for political transformation and the 'rebirth of Europe'. However, there is absolutely no sign that these ideas are moving out of the elitist ghetto in which they were conceived. As for paramilitary and electoral fascism, if this has no prospect of conquering power in present day Germany or Russia, despite the profound structural problems they are experiencing, what possible chance could any form of British fascism have of breaking through?

Admittedly fears of a new wave of immigration (e.g. from Hong Kong) compounded by particularly acute local socioeconomic grievances generated by Britain's inexorable industrial decline might conceivably allow a British fascist party to gather significant grassroots support in particular electoral wards. This would doubtless unleash a brief spate of moral panic among liberals and revolutionary expectations among socialist activists in the way that the election of Derek Beackon as a local councillor for Tower Hamlets did in the autumn of 1993. Such a scenario would be, in fact, a duplication of the conditions which allowed the National Front to gain a high media profile as Britain's fourth largest electoral party in the 1970s. It was a surge of public support for overtly racist policies which led the journalist Martin Walker to speculate in 1977 that 'in a period of crisis and uncertainty, a maverick party such as the NF could conceivably explode into power', and express the fear that the NF was 'reasonably well-equipped to take advantage of whatever political opportunities [the] future may yet offer them' (Walker, 1977, pp. 11–12). In retrospect such a judgement seems perversely wide of the mark. It could only be made by someone who took no account of the structural forces which have persistently ghettoized fascism even in deeply flawed liberal democracies, and thus was lured into endorsing the wild overestimation of their revolutionary potential characteristic of most extra-systemic political factions.

As for the academic perspective, the much more rigorous analysis of the National Front's place in English politics published by Stan Taylor five years later, when the party's terminal decline and self-destruction after the fiasco of the 1979 general election was already apparent, was able to report that his findings upheld the thesis 'that the English remain relatively immune to extremism' (Taylor, 1982, p. xvii). Even in this observation, however, Taylor, like Benewick before him, betrays an almost Whiggish belief that immunity to fascism is a characteristic of British political culture, rather than a structural feature of all but the most defective liberal democracies anywhere in the world. More recently a more sophisticated multicausal analysis of the failure of the extreme right in Britain was offered by Roger Eatwell. But here too a comparative perspective is missing, which may account for the debatable conclusion that even if 'in the short run, the extreme right's electoral prospects look bleak, . . . in the longer run, there is more than the glimmer of a new dawn' (Eatwell, 1992, p. 191).

In contrast, when British fascism is considered as a local manifestation of a generic phenomenon, such a new dawn seems destined never to get much beyond a faint glow on the horizon. It is just conceivable that a quirk of contemporary history might produce a fascist counterpart to the encouraging results obtained by the Greens in the Euro-elections of 1989, thus raising palingenetic expectations among the rank-and-file. But, as Greens too have found to their cost, even such a freak result still fails to bring an anti-systemic movement any closer to forming a regime and inaugurating a new order, the only achievement which fascists would regard as true 'success'. Not that die-hard fascists themselves would ever be put off by anything as trivial as repeated electoral disasters. The secret weapon in their psychological armoury is their palingenetic myth of imminent national rebirth. It is a myth which not only feeds off the minutest crumbs of hope (such as doubling a vote from 1.2 per cent to 2.4 per cent), but actually transforms even the most crushing setbacks into the harbingers of imminent triumph. It is a myth impervious to historical facts. Nevertheless, in the world constituted by those facts, no matter how ardently awaited, revolutionary sunrises, green, black (or red), turn out inevitably to have been a flash in the pan. The element of false analogy here is that the palingenetic hopes of (non-fascist) Greens for a new world order at least have a scientific basis in their diagnosis of current dysfunctions within the ecosystem, and once the unsustainability of the present system can no longer be ignored by a critical mass of political and economic elites, some sort of Green revolution is at least conceivable. By contrast, to imagine a conjuncture of events in which an overtly anti-liberal, hyper-nationalist, and revolutionary political force such as fascism might come to govern the country is to indulge not so much in counterfactual speculation as political science fiction.

CONCLUSION: THE PERPETUAL UGLY DUCKLING

One inference to be drawn from the above considerations is that it is a false point of departure to investigate the circumstances peculiar to British society which have enabled an effective tide-barrier to be erected against fascism's onslaught. There has never been a general spring tide of fascism threatening to burst the dikes of Western liberal or authoritarian regimes. In Britain its waters briefly swelled in the mid-1930s and the 1970s, but stayed low. It was only in inter-war Italy and Germany that fascism built up a head of pressure capable of breaching constitutional dikes already weakened by a nexus of illiberal factors, and even there the collapse was not an inevitability. Since then puddles and streams of fascism have formed in various countries, but memories of Fascism and Nazism should not lead us to overestimate either their depth or their destructive potential.

A corollary of this analysis is that it was not just Britain's long-established political culture of democratic consensus that neutralized the BUF in the 1930s, and is now neutralizing the BNP in the 1990s. All British fascisms are actually self-neutralizing due to the intrinsic weakness of the revolutionary threat they pose as permutations of palingenetic ultra-nationalism, and hence of an ideology which prescribes a total worldview and a programme of radical action which appeal naturally to a small minority. What marginalizes fascism, then, is the irreducible pluralism of modern society, and not the strength of liberalism as such, let alone the concerted opposition of anti-fascists inspired by the mobilizing myth provided by socialist analyses of the crisis of capitalism. To take just one example, it was not the election of the Conservative Party in 1979 that forestalled a National Front takeover of Britain, any more than it was the Anti-Nazi League that clipped its wings. Even left to its own devices the NF would have remained, like its rival the BNP, a minute, gawky, earthbound, ugly duckling destined to scratch around indefinitely without ever coming out as a swan.

Such a damning evaluation of the threat posed to modern democracy by the contemporary radical right is far from being a consensus view amongst journalists (the tone of *Searchlight*, for example, is consistently less sanguine), and would appear to be comparatively unusual amongst academics as well (see Prowe, 1994, p. 290). In the case of Britain, for example, Tony Kushner has recently offered a less complacent view of the significance of 'racism and neo-Nazism in contemporary Britain', although even he refers to the 'pitiful levels of fascist membership' and can only allude vaguely to the possibility of 'some sort of revival, if only on a small scale' (Kushner, 1994, p. 44). In as far as his article suggests that fascism and political racism are to be taken seriously as cankers on the face of any modern democracy, he is of course quite right. However pathetic the *revolutionary* threat posed by post-war fascism in Britain as elsewhere, this is not to say that the activities and permutations of British fascism do not need to be constantly monitored and combated by every democratic means available, both in its classic neo-Nazi manifestations and its various new discourses (New Right, Holocaust denial, Third Position, etc.: see Griffin, 1995, Part V). Its activists are certainly capable of whipping up a climate of racial hatred and violence in exceptional local conditions, and they occasionally still display the power to have blood on their hands if not on their conscience.

Fascism in Britain may be a storm in a tea-cup, but to individuals deemed by fascists 'un-British' and condemned to live in that tea-cup it is still a poisonous, potentially lethal brew, especially when stirred by openly terroristic formations such as the one which in the spring of 1995 engineered the riot which stopped the international football match between England and Ireland in Dublin. Fascist attempts to mobilize the forces of chauvinism and intolerance should thus be countered by every legal means available, both by the state and by voluntary activists and publicists. Indeed, there are arguments for banning fascist propaganda and activism which, by attacking the foundations of liberal society, by challenging the citizenship rights of ethnic minorities, or by reinforcing prejudices against traditional fascist targets (gays, Jews, gypsies, etc.), demonstrably incite violence and discrimination. The outlawing of BUF rallies and uniforms in 1936 and the internment of its members after war broke out could be seen as a healthy precedent for decisive action by a liberal state, just as much as the Weimar Republic's ban on the Nazi Party between November 1923 and February 1925, which was at least partially successful in preventing fascism from becoming a unified anti-democratic force in Germany. The contemporary German state continues to outlaw parties such as the Republicans once they are deemed to be 'extreme right' rather than just 'radical right', and Holocaust denial is a criminal offence, as Günther Deckert, leader of the neo-fascist National Democratic Party of Germany found to his cost.

Yet to go further and treat fascism as if it posed a realistic threat to the perpetuation of Britain's (albeit far from perfect) liberal democracy is to fall into the trap of taking at face value the fascists' own overestimation of their representativeness of popular sentiment and the imminence of their victory. Anti-fascist activists and scholars alike should beware of enhancing the credibility of the minute political constituency represented by true fascists by treating the genuine threat which fascists pose to social harmony and political stability in localized conditions as a revolutionary threat to the nation as a whole. The main risk which fascists pose to society, apart from the concrete acts of hatred and violence they inspire, is that of putting onto the agenda of mainstream politicians misgivings about the desirability or sustainability of a multi-ethnic, multi-faith society, and alarms about the contamination of alleged cultural 'purity' by foreign influence. Once such issues can be openly debated as genuine 'problems' requiring 'solutions', purportedly liberal states can come all too easily to collude with the forces of racism and ultra-nationalism. Thus it is that certain policies relating to immigration, citizenship and national identity adopted in Thatcher's Britain (see Eatwell, 1992), Kohl's Germany and Mitterrand's France in the last two decades can be seen in part as concessions to the influence of fears raised by extreme right propagandists.

It would be ironic indeed if political scientists could one day show that the spectre of fascism's success in the minds of anti-fascists and of politicians of the liberal right had achieved more influence on politics than 'actually existing fascism' itself, condemned indefinitely to remain a marginalized and ghettoized force in Britain as elsewhere, could ever have hoped for. Meanwhile, students of fascism and those concerned to expose and demystify its mythic claims would be advised not to ask 'why has British fascism always failed?' but 'what circumstances could conceivably materialize which might enable it to succeed?'

REFERENCES

Benewick, R., *The Fascist Movement in Britain* (London, 1971).
Cheles, L. et al., *Neo-fascism in Western Europe* (London, 1991).
Eatwell, R., 'Why has the extreme right failed in Britain?' in Hainsworth, P. (ed.), *The Extreme Right in Europe and the USA* (London, 1992).
Ford, G., *Fascist Europe* (London, 1992).
Griffin, R., *The Nature of Fascism* (London, 1993).
Griffin, R., *Fascism* (Oxford, 1995).
Hitler, A., *Mein Kampf* (London, 1939).
Kushner, T., 'The fascist as "other"? Racism and neo-Nazism in contemporary Britain', *Patterns of Prejudice*, Vol. 29, No. 1, 1994.
Lunn, K. and Thurlow, R., *British Fascism* (London, 1980).
Ó Maoláin, C., *The Radical Right: A World Directory* (London, 1987).
Platt, G.M., 'Thoughts on a theory of collective action: language, affect, and ideology in revolution', in Albin, M. (ed.), *New Directions in Psychohistory* (Lexington, Mass., 1980).
Prowe, D., '"Classic" fascism and the new radical right in Western Europe: comparisons and contrasts', *Contemporary European Politics*, Vol. 3, No. 3, 1994.
Rauschning, H., *Hitler Speaks* (London, 1939).
Schmidt, M., *The New Reich* (London, 1993).
Taylor, S., *The National Front in English Politics* (London, 1982).
Tyndall, J., *The Eleventh Hour: A Call for British Rebirth* (London, 1988).
Walker, M., *The National Front* (London, 1977).

9 British Fascism Revisited: A Failure of Imagination?
Kenneth Lunn

What remains to be said about the analysis of fascism in Britain in the twentieth century? Since the publication of the work of Cross and Benewick in the 1960s, it might be thought that the bones have been picked over fairly thoroughly and little of substance remains to be digested. However, the resurgence of fascism elsewhere in Europe, and the alarm bells sounded by the success of the British National Party in Tower Hamlets in 1993, have provided a trigger for some attempts at evaluating, at the end of the century, the nature of the British experience of fascism. There has certainly been a plenitude of studies on aspects of the National Front and on the British National Party and the holding of the conference at Sheffield Hallam University in 1994 was an indication of the continued academic interest in the topic.

However, in many ways, this interest in British fascism has not seen a comparable advance in the theoretical and methodological approaches to its study. What might now be defined as the standard text, Richard Thurlow's *Fascism in Britain* (1987), is the most quoted study in any discussion of the topic and its approach is the one most frequently cited in historical and political science literature. Yet, a careful perusal of Thurlow's work indicates its fairly conventional approach in terms of research and theoretical perspective and is thus a good indicator of both the strengths of the existing literature and its deficiencies.

It is not the intention of this closing chapter to replay a survey of the historiography in any great detail. A number of the other contributors in this volume have done that to good effect. What can be suggested about that historiography is that little of the developments in historical and sociological analysis over the last twenty years has made much impact on the study of British fascism. It is as if it has become locked into its own agenda and has ignored or failed to engage fully with general trends in the various disciplines from which it draws its expertise. Whilst Thurlow and others have trawled extensively in the body of released material in the Public Record Office and produced a series of articles and books based around these sources, the essential interpretation of British fascism has remained fairly constant. The emphasis of research and publication is upon the perceived major players – the British Union of Fascists, Oswald Mosley, the National Front and the leading figures in that organization. Most attention is devoted to the central core of these parties and to their activities at a national level and in electoral politics. Given this kind of context, it is hardly surprising that many of the writers have found it relatively easy to see British fascism as doomed to failure and as relatively insignificant within an overall study of British political ideologies. The priority of explanatory factors for this failure to make a significant impact may vary from account to account but the essential checklist of items remains the same. The lack of social, economic and political crisis comparable to that of Germany or Italy in the inter-war period, the absence of genuinely charismatic and populist leaders, the problems associated with the more deeply rooted political affiliations and institutions of the British system – these are the main elements in most standard accounts.

These dimensions are undoubtedly important and, examined with the kind of thoroughness appropriate to any historical, political or sociological analysis, will continue to provide a core element in any understanding of the nature of British fascism. However, it does seem that the citing of such factors as identified above has become a substitute for critical analysis. It is as if the assumptions which have often lain behind this kind of approach to the study of British fascism have become established political 'facts', rather than assumptions or hypotheses. As D.S. Lewis has pointed out, perhaps the most obvious illustration of this is the somewhat caricatured version of an argument that fascism in Britain was eliminated '... by the moderation and tolerance of the British character or culture' (Lewis, 1987, p. 261). Lewis goes on to make a most vehement challenge to this notion and the assumptions behind its approach, and is particularly scathing about its methodological laziness:

> In reality neither nations nor races have inherent common traits of character. Nor even is there such an entity as a single national culture. Nations are no more than arbitrary lines drawn upon maps containing individuals and groups of individuals with competing interests and incompatible needs and aspirations. Certainly there were differences in the historical development of individual nations, but to suggest that there were any unique elements within British society, which made it immune to the threat of fascism, is to illustrate an extraordinary complacency founded upon misplaced arrogance.
>
> (Lewis, 1987, p. 261)

While not necessarily agreeing with every single nuance of Lewis's critique, there are significant points raised here which seem to have been largely undervalued or unappreciated by academics working in the field. Some of the points raised will be returned to in the pages that follow.

Above all, what Lewis seems to have been asking for was a more radical rethinking of the ways in which to understand and to analyse British fascism. It is with similar intentions that the various contributors to this volume have sought to explore a number of areas and to challenge, in some cases, the conventional wisdom of the existing literature. It is the intention of this chapter to examine briefly the areas of discussion opened up by the preceding chapters, before relating the material to other recent studies on British fascism and ending with an attempt to set out a critical agenda for future research and methodological approaches to the topic.

In overall terms, it may be that the most stimulating approach for future work is that of Roger Griffin (Griffin, 1993). His theoretical work in recent years has provided a framework for progressive discussion of the nature of fascism and his contribution to this volume provides a much wider contextual model for the consideration of the 'failure' of British fascism. By highlighting the inability of fascism to achieve political power in most nation-states throughout the twentieth century, Griffin has suggested that the emphasis on explaining the failure has been a kind of self-fulfilling prophecy and that it may be more valuable to pursue positive questions about where, when and why it was able to make an impact, in Britain as elsewhere.

Again, it is not crucial to accept all of Griffin's characterization or conclusions to be able to use his approach to extend any discussion.

More specifically, the other studies focus on a number of stages in the chronology of British fascism. Baker and Thurlow examine all aspects of the inter-war period, providing a re-evaluation of the marginalization of the phenomenon in the 1920s and more evidence of the extent and nature of the British state's control and monitoring of the BUF and its adherents. Both of these studies align themselves with the weight of existing interpretation on the inter-war years and offer detailed explanations of fascism's inability to move beyond defined political margins.

The work on the post-war period provides a range of evidence and interpretation. Anne Poole's discussion of the ways in which European networking developed in the immediate post-war years is a timely reminder that fascism, as with many other political ideologies, knows no political boundaries and that attempts to define national traditions and features must always be conscious of the transmission of ideas and aspirations across frontiers. The three other contributors, Eatwell, Durham and Copsey, direct their attention to the post 1960s-period of organized politics and, while examining different elements of the fascist movement, all seek to move the debate beyond the standard interpretation. In particular both Durham and Copsey employ very effectively the notion of 'political space', analysing ways in which fascists and other political parties create the kind of discourses and agendas which encourage the promotion of fascist values and support for such politics. Such ideas are not, however, new, although the conceptual language and approach has become more sophisticated. In a study of Wolverhampton politics, Jones identified the post-First World War political vacuum in particular wards which allowed groups such as ex-servicemen, communists and fascists to compete quite effectively for the ideological high ground and for electoral support (Jones, 1969, pp. 87–8). This concept of political space, which clearly is not limited to a discussion of the ability to contest parliamentary or local elections, is one which may offer one of the most significant methodological tools for grappling with the complexities of British fascism in the twentieth century.

The second theme of this chapter is to identify how more recent work has opened up the discussion of British fascism. As already suggested, much has continued to plough the same furrows but there have been significant diversions from that established path. In particular, it has been the case that local studies have produced the most valuable advances. This is not simply because in most cases they fulfil the somewhat antiquarian history criterion of 'adding to knowledge' but because the range of sources and the methodology of social history and of sociological analysis are most readily employed in this kind of work. Studies of fascism at this level are, therefore, much more open than traditional political history approaches seem to allow. Nigel Copsey's exploration of the Tower Hamlets situation in this volume is an excellent illustration of the strengths of this kind of research. It provides us with worked examples of the construction of a discourse on race and the politicization of these issues, explaining how a local political culture, albeit one which is shaped to a degree by a 'national' agenda, can be receptive to some of the ideological concerns of fascism. This would appear to provide a far greater understanding, and a more dynamic model, than any assertion about the nature of 'British' political culture can provide.

Other local studies on historical dimensions of British fascism have also indicated further avenues of research. One of the most significant insights highlights the linkages between allegedly distinctive political ideologies and organizations, in particular the lack of division between mainstream right-wing politics and fascism. Whilst this is a topic which has been identified in earlier writings, notably that of Richard Griffiths (1983), Gerry Webber (1986) and David Cesarani (1989), the tendency has been to accept the Arnold Leese interpretation of linkages as 'Conservatism with Knobs on' rather than as 'Conservative fascism', as is suggested below. Indeed, reading beyond the conventional literature on fascism as such, provides evidence of the potential for a more careful perspective on 'political blurring'. Martin Pugh has written, albeit briefly, on the possible cross-over between Conservatives and fascism in the 1930s:

> Though ostensibly confronting the left, the BUF competed with the right for support. The fears, for instance, of

Conservative MPs about loss of young patriots to Mosley in the early 1930s is corroborated by the urgent requests made by the Primrose League habitations for guidance on the whole subject of fascism.

(Pugh, 1985, p. 191)

This emphasis seems important and one which could be fruitfully pursued. In their local studies, both David Turner (1993) and Thomas Linehan (1993) have noted for the inter-war period the association between fascism and the Conservative Party. In both areas, evidence is provided of the ways in which unsettled individuals found their own political aspirations and objectives being frustrated or thwarted and thus sought to shift their allegiance without necessarily altering their political convictions and aspirations.

Turner's study of the Medway towns shows connections between the Conservative Party and the British Fascists in the 1920s, as well as expressions of support for Franco's Spain from the Conservative MP for Gillingham and 'favourable references to Hitler' by the man who later became Conservative MP for Canterbury. The commonality of interest between local Conservatives and the British Fascists in the 1920s centred around the opposition to 'communists', a term which covered those who were members of the Communist Party and also a range of others identified as 'fellow travellers'. It was a degree of passion and of ultra-patriotism which produced some very active challenges towards 'the Reds' (Turner, 1993, pp. 8–10) and a blurring of the political distinction between mainstream right and radical right. Turner himself has suggested that the appearance of some elements of the British Fascists gave the impression of 'something of a joke organisation' (Turner, 1993, p. 10) but he clearly sees them as having created a basis from which the BUF was able to launch its own political programme in the 1930s.

Evidence of support for Francoism and for Hitler's Germany provided in Turner's study reinforces the kinds of evidence produced in Griffiths' work and repeated in others. In this sense, it offers nothing new. What it does indicate is the way in which political agendas could coincide and how Conservatives and fascists could play off each other's public pronouncements and political perspectives. It also provides some evidence of overlapping membership and of the easy shift between organizations. It is this kind of evidence which directly challenges the political scientist approach of tight definitions of fascism and traditional right ideologies and parties. At a local level, the lived political experiences of those who operated on the political right refused to be bound by such conceptualizations and we ought to acknowledge ways in which these boundaries were crossed in the inter-war years.

Linehan's study equally indicates this kind of elision. In looking at Hackney and Stoke Newington in London, he indicates the fascist sympathies of some local Conservatives, who sometimes operated under the guise of the United Ratepayers or Municipal Reform (Linehan, 1993, pp. 151–3). The support of the local Stoke Newington Grocers' Association for an anti-Jewish lobby also helped stimulate a public discourse fuelled by fascist activity in the district. There are also hints about the 'Conservative fascism' of the Central Hackney branch of the BUF. This phrase used by Linehan is presumably a carefully chosen one and offers a rarely spoken concept for further investigation. What it does is open further the discussion of ideological differences within the BUF and of close links between some aspects of its ideological approach and certainly of elements of the membership and the more mainstream parties.

This indication is further supported by Nigel Todd's work on fascism in the North East (Todd, 1995). For him, whatever the assessment of the impact of the British Fascists in the 1920s might be:

> ... it foretold several fault-lines of a native Fascism: preservation of private property rights, a preoccupation with the officer-class, gross self-importance and reciprocal jealousy, a willingness to engage in paramilitary violence and, underpinning all of these, racial and political hatreds. These ideas could be found throughout the British Right in the inter-war decades, but Fascists took them, to nightmarish proportions.
> (Todd, 1995, pp. 6–7)

Perhaps not overtly, what Todd is indicating is the need to rethink the whole conception of right-wing politics in twentieth-century Britain.

Finally, then, what of a new agenda for research on British

fascism? As has already been outlined, there does appear to be a certain reluctance to draw upon the debates and theoretical perspectives found elsewhere in British academia, although some honourable exceptions to this have been cited. What are those weaknesses in existing literature?

Perhaps the biggest barrier to any different understanding of the impact of fascism in Britain is a failure of the imagination. This is not an argument for the extensive use of 'counterfactual' history, since by definition that operates within the realms of speculation and cannot replace the detailed analysis of attitudes and events which are available to the historian. The somewhat smug notion, however, that Britain, or British society, was somehow immune to the tendency to support or sympathize with fascist regimes needs to be shaken. Recent studies of Vichy France and of the Channel Islands during the Second World War have provided ample illustration of the ways in which societies perceived to have firm roots in democratic politics have fallen into line with many aspects of fascism. The argument does not need to be carried to the extreme of what would have happened if Britain had been invaded and occupied in 1940 by the Nazis in order to develop this line of discussion. Such speculation is at worst fictional. What is apparent is that British society cannot be simply assumed to be devoid of elements of sympathy for the ideological dimensions of fascist activity. It is vital for historians not simply to ask why fascism failed but also to enquire about its successes. To do this requires an open mind, a historical imagination, and an ability and a willingness not to close down avenues of enquiry. This has not always been to the fore in the historical writing on British fascism.

All this is not to suggest that a historical imagination will construct a vision of fascism's impact, which is a distortion of what is palpably the case. There is a tendency, often based on current political concerns, to exaggerate the historical significance of fascism in Britain. Any 'revisionist' approach lays itself open to this tendency. What has been lacking in much recent historiography is a failure to engage with the range of historical methodology and social and political analysis. A wider frame of reference for considering both political failure and success is vital, one that does not see the ballot box as the sole criteria for assessment. We also need to avoid, or perhaps more importantly analyse, notions of British political culture and British liberal tradition, phrases which have been increasingly used as mantras in the recitation of fascism's failure. Long before the onset of post-modernism, we should have been asking in this context: 'What exactly is British political culture?' Is it valid to identify a single dominating ethos or should we be recognizing and analysing the existence of different patterns of political behaviour and forms of construction? Should we not be seeing 'political culture' as a dynamic rather than as a fixed entity, where the watertight compartments of some political science conceptualization clearly restricts our evaluation of political behaviour and attempts to package it neatly into forms which do not correspond to the 'real' experience and attitudes of political actors?

Thus, statements such as:

> No-one wastes any time in explaining why such quixotic and eccentric movements such as the British Fascisti in the 1920s and the Imperial Fascist League in the 1930s were minute elements on the political fringes.
> (Thurlow, 1989, p. 67)

ought not go unchallenged. Such an approach is both negative and dangerous in terms of any notion of a more subtle appreciation of the impact of fascism in Britain.

First, it gives credence to the notion that fascism is a foreign import, an influence alien to British political tradition and thus doomed to failure. The use of words like 'quixotic' and 'eccentric' emphasize this kind of approach. It leads ultimately to the sort of conclusion which does not need to explain the failure of fascism: its collapse is self-evident and self-fulfilling.

Second, it reinforces the view that fascism's impact can be measured solely in terms of membership of organizations and by its ability to contest elections at local and national level. While analyses of the National Front have sometimes been prepared to recognize the ways in which the party influenced a wider political agenda on issues such as 'race', immigration and law and order, historians of the pre-Second World War fascisms have been strangely reluctant to acknowledge similar possibilities.

Third, the general tone of the quotation from Thurlow's work indicates a narrowness of focus, an attempt to close down areas of interpretation which may still offer more fruitful approaches to the study of British fascism.

Finally, it seems to suggest that the lived history and contemporary experiences of fascism, particularly where they concern only relatively small groups of people, are unimportant. As such, it displays an elitism which cannot be helpful for the advancement of any understanding of the nature and impact of fascism in Britain. All four of these themes can be developed in more detail.

Fascism as a foreign import

Fascism is above all associated with Mussolini's Italy and Hitler's Germany. However much academic research seeks to widen the net, both geographically and chronologically, inevitable comparisons are made with these regimes. This has profound methodological complications in terms of defining fascism as an ideology and in terms of the theoretical problems of constructing a typology which can respond to the range of regimes and movements which may be seen as deserving of the label. Roger Griffin's work, in this volume and elsewhere, which has certainly advanced significantly the debate on this theoretical level, is still drawn towards this comparative approach.

In the case of Britain, this frequently means that the British version of fascism is identified as an importation, as a pale imitation of the full-bloodied version in Nazi Germany or Fascist Italy. The ways in which this notion is pursued vary considerably. There are the somewhat crude representations of the British Fascists in the 1920s as motivated solely by the emergence of fascism in Italy. Equally there are the studies of Oswald Mosley which emphasize his contacts with Mussolini and Hitler and seem to stress these relationships as the driving force behind the British Union of Fascists. In addition, the Anti-Nazi League in the 1970s campaigned on the platform of linking key figures and ideas in the National Front with the politics and culture of Nazi Germany. As a political strategy, this may have had a degree of success but it also helped to reinforce the idea that fascism in Britain was the product of admiration and aping of Nazi Germany, rather than the product of any native tradition. Michael Billig's work on the National Front (Billig, 1978) was damning in its focus on the parallels between aspects of ideology and of organization of the Nazis. It fitted, however, the typology which identified British fascism as imitative. Again, there are sound reasons for such an approach and the kinds of evidence which Billig and others drew upon made such conclusions sustainable. It is still the case, however, that they could help to deny the importance of examining the British roots of British fascism.

Of course, it would be foolish to argue that British fascism was conceived and developed in a political vacuum or that it did not draw upon other versions in its evolution. Indeed, it would be wrong to argue that any political movement or regime was not part of a wider context and series of influences. However, the main point of this discussion is to reinforce the idea that there exists within whatever is defined as British political culture a degree of sympathy for the forms of political behaviour espoused by British fascist movements. Somewhat naively, perhaps, this has been referred to as a native tradition of British fascism. Whilst this may be a crude labelling and conceptualization, it deserves closer attention. Many standard texts, however, refuse to engage with this notion, seeing anything before Oswald Mosley and the BUF as insignificant in every sense or, in the case of Thurlow and Lewis, make gestural efforts to deal with antecedents without a great deal of commitment. David Baker's approach in this volume seems to reinforce this line of thinking. While it has a logic of its own, it is unlikely to advance an understanding of the complex processes of fascism's history, as a movement and as an ideology throughout the twentieth century.

Measures of fascism's political impact

For far too long, the gauge of fascism's success has been the lack of parliamentary representation, paltry numbers of local councillors, relatively few votes and membership figures which bear no comparison to those of other political parties in Britain and which fail to match those of Nazi Germany and Fascist Italy. Measured by such criteria, it is very simple to dismiss fascism's significance.

However, the limitations of such a narrow definition of political 'success' are many. Taking this approach is representative of a very elitist view of historical analysis or political sociology.

In other areas of these disciplines, and in somewhat different approaches to the study of the subject matter, a more wide-ranging and sophisticated analysis has long been employed. Surely debates, decisions and actions at a national level or within the core of the leadership can no more constitute the sum total of fascism's significance than for any political movement or party? Would it be seen as legitimate to discuss the impact of the Labour Party in the 1920s purely in terms of its parliamentary activities? While some texts have adopted this approach, they have been quite effectively challenged for the narrowness of focus.

It is also vital that we do not narrow the focus of research and concern ourselves solely with traditional sources and traditional interpreters of that material. Indeed some of the most challenging of ideas in recent years have come not from established historians or political scientists but from journalists and literary figures. Arguably, Kazuo Ishiguro's recent novel (Ishiguro, 1989) has more to say about the social and psychological aspects of 1930s fascism in Britain that any number of academic histories.

'The end of history?'

It surely cannot be sustainable to argue that particular aspects of study in the field of British fascism should now be considered as academic 'no-go areas'. Authors such as John Hope have already provided evidence of the complex relationships between fascism, the 'establishment' and state organizations (Hope, 1992) and even Thurlow has indicated that much material in the possession of the state has yet to be made available for public scrutiny (Thurlow, 1995). Access to MI5 and Special Branch files might produce some startling revelations. However, even if it could be argued that all the evidence has been uncovered, that should not preclude continuing to think about and to interpret such evidence. The notion that we no longer have anything to say about any particular aspect of British fascism's history runs counter to most academic traditions of investigation. It is tantamount to arguing that once all the facts have been discovered, a history is complete, a methodology long since discredited.

As Roger Griffin has argued, particular nation-states and

organizations retain their individual forms and significance in terms of the fascist movements which emerge within any generic typology. Equally, it is possible to argue that any real understanding of how and where fascism seizes hold can only be achieved through the kind of detailed research undertaken on Nazi Germany and Fascist Italy. National perspectives, in this sense, can hinder the processes of research.

The importance of 'lived' history

A range of assumptions seem explicit in such a history. There is the elitist aspect – the notion that only 'significant' figures and organizations are deserving of close attention and therefore of their own history. As has already been suggested, this notion of the predominance of so-called mainstream history and politics exposes the predilection towards a top-down approach. As academics, we cannot therefore afford to ignore the complexities of groups and the individuals who comprise those groups, the processes whereby they arrive at particular patterns of thinking and the reasons for their support of ideologies and organizations, however minuscule their impact on national and international politics may be deemed to be. There are significances in such processes which can be analysed and drawn upon and ought not to be neglected. To assume that only major groups and individuals count is a display of liberal arrogance and a dismissal which will only ultimately weaken our ability to understand and explain the phenomenon of fascism.

It also detracts from very important aspects of fascism: the personal significance for those whose lives were affected by the social and political doctrines and by the actions of those involved with fascism. As Roger Griffin has argued in this volume, 'Fascism in Britain may be a storm in a tea-cup, but to individuals deemed by fascists "un-British" and condemned to live in that tea-cup, it is still a poisonous, potentially lethal brew.'

Griffin's remarks are clearly a reference to the most recent objects of fascist and racist violence in Britain but they are equally valid for those who were on the receiving end of fascist hatred in the inter-war years. The pressures, mental and physical, experienced by considerable numbers of British citizens over the years should not be obscured by an obsession with grand history.

Naturally, this is a personalized view of avenues of future research and problems associated with existing approaches. If it is critical of work in the past, this is a reflection of the desire to push forward and to stimulate debate on a topic which is not simply of academic interest but which has a powerful and threatening political significance for many groups in contemporary Britain. It is with the aim of a greater understanding and awareness that the plea for an opening up of discussion is made. Perhaps the notion of the failure of British fascism is a dangerous one to pursue? Roger Griffin's warning not to exaggerate the threat posed by fascism to 'the nation as a whole' is well taken but, equally, we cannot assume that there exists an impermeable barrier between so-called conventional politics and those of fascism. The historical evidence of the dangers of such assumptions are still very obvious and to parallel the arguments of some extreme right revisionists would seem to be a route fraught with considerable perils.

REFERENCES

Benewick, R.J., *The Fascist Movement in Britain* (London, 1971).
Billig, M., *Fascists: A Social Psychological View of the National Front* (London, 1978).
Cesarani, D., 'Joynson-Hicks and the radical right in England after the First World War', in Kushner, T. and Lunn, K. (eds), *Traditions of Intolerance: Historical Perspectives on Fascism and Race Discourse in Britain* (Manchester, 1989).
Cross, C., *The Fascists in Britain* (London, 1961).
Griffin, R., *Fellow Travellers of the Right* (London, 1983).
Griffin, R., *The Nature of Fascism* (London, 1991).
Hope, J., 'British fascism and the state, 1917–27: a re-examination of the documentary evidence', *Labour History Review*, Vol. 57, No. 3, 1992.
Ishiguro, K., *The Remains of the Day* (London, 1989).
Jones, G.W., *Borough Politics: A Study of the Wolverhampton Town Council, 1888–1964* (London, 1969).
Lewis, G.W., *Illusions of Grandeur: Mosley, Fascism and British Society, 1931–81* (Manchester, 1987).
Linehan, T., 'The British Union of Fascists in Hackney and Stoke Newington, 1933–40', in Alderman, G. and Holmes, C. (eds), *Outsiders and Outcasts: Essays in Honour of William J. Fishman* (London, 1993).
Pugh, M., *The Tories and the People, 1880–1935* (Oxford, 1985).

Thurlow, R., *Fascism in Britain: A History, 1918–85* (Oxford, 1987).
Thurlow, R., 'The failure of British Fascism', in Thorpe, A. (ed.), *The Failure of Political Extremism in Inter-War Britain* (Exeter, 1989).
Thurlow, R., *The Secret State: British Internal Security in the Twentieth Century* (Oxford, 1995).
Todd, N., *In Excited Times: The People Against the Blackshirts* (Whitley Bay, 1995).
Turner, D., *Fascism and Anti-Fascism in the Medway Towns, 1927–1940* (Rochester, 1993).
Webber, G.C., *The Ideology of the British Right, 1918–1939* (London, 1986).
Webber, G.C., 'Intolerance and discretion: Conservatives and British Fascism, 1918–1926', in Kushner, T. and Lunn, K. (eds), *Traditions of Intolerance: Historical Perspectives on Fascism and Race Discourse in Britain* (Manchester, 1989).

Index

Amery, John, 29
Anderson, Ian, 113
anti-immigration, 63, 83–4, 94, 125–34
Anti-Nazi League, 163, 175
anti-Semitism, 16, 17–20, 21, 23, 25, 42–3, 44, 100
Armed Revolutionary Nuclei (Italy), 111
Association of Jewish Ex-Servicemen, 58

Battle of Cable Street, 35, 41, 46
Bean, John, 81, 86
Beackon, Derek, 125, 134
Beamish, Henry Hamilton, 18
Beckman, Maurice, 59
Big Brothers League, 16
Bilderberg Group, 85–7
Board of Deputies of British Jews, 44
Bolshevik Revolution 1917, 13, 17
British Democratic Party, 82, 96, 120
British Fascists, 16, 19–21, 30–1, 152
British League of Ex-Servicemen, 57, 61
British Movement, 59, 81, 105, 120
British National Fascisti, 21
British National Party, 5, 82, 97, 106, 118–39, 144, 160, 163; electoral politics, 121–2, 124–34
British National Socialist Movement, 126
British Union of Fascists, 5, 29, 32, 40–2, 47, 54, 56, 143–4, 152–6, 175
Britons Society, 18
Brons, Andrew, 113
Butler, Eddy, 135

Chesterton, A.K., 16, 81, 83–4, 86–8, 93, 114

Childs, Sir Wyndham, 30
collaboration, 173
Column 88, 103
Combat 18, 2, 136
Communist Party of Great Britain, 24, 29–30, 32, 37, 40, 44, 57–8
Conservative Party, 23–4, 83–4, 94–5, 103, 162–3

Defence Unions, 18, 30
Diehards, 15–16, 18

18b Detainees (British) Fund, 56, 61
European Social Movement, 76–9

failure, conditions and reasons for, 2, 7–8, 22–6, 49–51, 54, 65–8, 97–8, 100–2, 115–16, 120, 122–4, 137–9, 141–2, 152–65
fascism, comparative European movements, 153–6, 157–9, 175–6; conditions for success, 4–5, 145–6; crisis, 147–9; definitions, 6–7, 121, 142–3, 167–9; impact of, 176–7; origins in Britain, 17; political space for, 146–7, 169–70
The Fascist, 21, 43
Flag Group of the National Front, 112–15
'43 Group (later '62 Group), 59
Fountaine, Andrew, 81–2

Game, Sir Philip, 36, 38–9, 43, 45
Greater Britain Movement, 81
Griffin, Nick, 111

Hamm, Jeffrey, 57
Harrington, Patrick, 111
Hawkins, Neil Francis, 21
Hitler, Adolf, 150
Holland, Derek, 109, 111
housing and race, 128–33

Index

Imperial Fascist League, 21, 43
internment, 50-1, 54-6
Italian fascism, 151-2

January Club, 32
Jewish People's Congress, 44
Joyce, William, 21, 29

Knight, Maxwell, 30-2, 48

League of Empire Loyalists, 55, 81, 114
Liberal Democrats, 125-34
Leese, Arnold, 21, 43-4, 69
local studies of British fascism, 170-2

Marconi scandal, 15-16
media, and the British National Party, 118-19, 121-4, 136-7; and the British Union of Fascists, 33-4; and Combat 18, 2; and the National Front, 101
MI5, 30-1, 34, 40-1, 47
Monday Club, 8, 83, 89-93
Mosley, Sir Oswald, 1, 31, 32, 42, 48-9, 53-4, 57, 60, 61-8, 99; links with European fascisms, 73-9; political thinking, 68-79

National Council for Civil Liberties, 34, 44-5, 58
National Democratic Party, 86
National Front, 5, 81, 93-8, 99-116, 120, 160, 162-3, 175-6
National Front Constitutional Movement, 82, 96
National Party, 17, 81-2, 86
Nazism, 151-2
New National Front, 82, 106, 120
North Kensington election 1959, 63-4
Nouvelle Droite, 108

Olympia Meeting 1934, 32, 41
Orman, Rotha Lintorn, 19, 21, 31

parliamentary tradition, 5, 22, 25-6
The Patriot, 16, 19
Political Soldiers, 112-15
Powell, Enoch, 83, 84-9
Protocols of the Elders of Zion, 17
Public Order Act 1936, 34-5, 36, 39, 44, 46-7, 62, 164

race violence, 63, 104-5, 129, 139
racist supremacy, 70-2
revisionism, of holocaust, 100; of Nuremberg trials, 74-5

Skrewdriver, 104
Smith, Steve, 124-5
Spearhead, 119
Special Branch, 29-30, 34, 40-1

Taylor, James, 57
Thatcher, Margaret, 83, 94-5, 103, 107
Tower Hamlets election, September 1993, 1-2, 118-19, 124-34; May 1994, 134
Trenchard, Lord, 35-8, 40
Tyndall, John, 9, 81, 83, 84-6, 89, 95, 99, 106, 115, 120-5, 135, 137, 145

Union Movement, 5, 53, 56, 60, 61-8, 99

Walker, Michael, 108
Webster, Martin, 81, 83, 86, 88, 92, 99, 106-7

Yellow Star Movement, 59